MW01166383

Hotel Renovation

Planning & Design

Hotel Renovation

Planning & Design

Frederic Knapp

RETAIL REPORTING CORP., NEW YORK

Retail Reporting Corporation
302 Fifth Avenue
New York, NY 10001

Distributors to the trade in the United States and Canada
McGraw-Hill, Inc
1221 Avenue of the Americas
New York, NY 10020

Distributors outside the United States and Canada
Hearst Books International
1350 Avenue of the Americas
New York, NY 10019

Library of Congress Cataloging in Publication Data:
Hotel Renovation Planning & Design

Printed in Hong Kong
ISBN 0-934590-58-3

Designed: Mira Zivkovich, Inc.

C o n t e n t s

Introduction

Depending on how closely you look, hospitality renovation projects may all look the same -or so different there's no resemblance among them. Leaf through the "before" photos showing the results of previous renovations of the hotels in this book, and you'll find you can date them with ease. Current projects seem to cover the entire spectrum of style, but it's safe to say that in twenty years, they'll start to look a lot more similar to one another. So maybe all renovations in a given period are really the same. On the other hand, read the details behind the projects, and it may seem that each renovation team had to reinvent the wheel. The budget project scope, the micro-market conditions are as divergent from case to case as the existing buildings themselves. Maybe there's no common thread beyond the given of hotel and renovation.

Despite the apparently limitless variables, some important constant emerge when renovation is viewed from a greater distance. every owner or operator has to answer the same questions in renovating a property. first, how much can be spent, and when will the design and construction be performed? Will the work be done in phases, and will operations continue during construction? What choices does the market offer - and what changes does it demand? What regulatory and building code requirements apply? What will be the make-up of the renovation team, and who will really lead it? And finally, what should guests notice most once the project is complete?

Renovation projects can be divided into some broad categories, based on the answer to these questions and characteristics of the properties themselves. A hotel like the Hyatt Regency New Orleans that is doing well in a stable market does not need to be reinvented, and its renovation will be accordingly long on furniture, finishes and equipment and short on gutting of partitions. It isn't critical that such a makeover break new ground; it just has to keep the property fresh and avoid throwing anything off balance. At the other end of the spectrum, the new owner of a previously unsuccessful property like the Houstonian or the Equinox is bound to make a bold change. Where the failed operation lacked focus, the challenge is to pinpoint a market strategy and reshape the physical plant to do it. Ideally, a major renovation will guarantee the owner a market reposition, but there is a difference between enhancing rates after an ambitious renovation and getting an entirely different clientele, as the owner of the Washington, D.C. Courtyard by Marriott did. Every renovation makes property improvements, but a reposition must radically improve design and materials while changing the basic product itself. Resurrections of long-closed hotels like the Omni-Severin, the Hotel Macdonald, and the Governor and conversions like the Broadway American and the Vintage Plaza impose no burden on the renovation team of coordinating construction with current operations, but they do impose the constriction of working with an existing building - without the benefit of an established clientele already loyal to the property. Last but not least among the types of renovations are projects which refine and evolve an ongoing operation, changing it noticeably but not radically. At the Arizona Biltmore, renovating meant carefully adjusting minor details in public spaces, adding new facilities and augmenting specific services significantly, but only fine-tuning the overall character of the property. Hilton Hawaiian Village with 2,500 rooms, from high-rise towers and a score of smaller buildings, is too huge to be transformed; a phased master plan reshaped key aspects of the property, adjusting its direction the way a helmsman steers an ocean liner.

One type of hotel worth mentioning in particular - not necessarily a classification of renovation - is the historic property. Customer loyalty, marketing cachet, local permit approvals and federal tax credits strongly influence the renovation team to retain and restore important features which make a building historic. While restoring nearly every space to its original condition is practical for a small property like the Bancroft Hotel, larger ones have to strike a compromise between restoration and renovation. Seen purely from the balance sheet, adding a tower with hundreds of new guest rooms would have been the crowning glory of the renovation of San Francisco's Sheraton Palace; in the historical perspective returning the building exactly to what it was in 1909 would have been the ultimate feat. Neither approach ultimately carried the day, but elements of each have made the renovation successful, both on the balance sheets and in the public eye.

Important commonalities exist in the renovation process, even where the properties and the projects are quite different. The owner and operator must decide a clear goal for the renovation, using their knowledge of the property and market conditions. In choosing architects, interior designers, contractors, construction managers and renovation advisers, owners and operators almost invariably opt for individuals and firms with similar experiences - and preferably personal experience. The outside members of the team must find working methods that are comfortable for the owner and operator, and the owner and operator have to give a vote of confidence to the rest of the team. With such a solid foundation, the project can get off to a good start at the beginning of the design phase; all parties should be ready to make major decisions as soon as they are needed - and be flexible in changing them whenever conditions warrant. While compatibility and cooperation are essential, leadership is also indispensable. Successful renovations come from owners and operators with a strong sense of where the property should head, architects and interior designers with a clear vision of the finished project and a construction team that knows just how to build it.

All this adds up to a successful project, but what makes a project worth looking at in a book? A daring or unusual design approach - if it's successful - can't fail to elicit interest. Ironically a design that sums up what is going on everywhere is also noteworthy, simply for being an archetype of its age. Unusual properties, distinctive buildings and out-of-the-ordinary renovation goals and noteworthy project delivery methods also make interesting studies.

Frederic Knapp

Hotel Renovation
Planning & Design

Hotel Inter-Continental
Chicago, Illinois

Chicago boomed in the 1920s, even some of the proudest Midwesterners couldn't help envying the mystery and intrigue of the Old World, so they created buildings like the Shriners' Medinah Athletic Club. If they had seen it at the time, Evelyn Waugh or H. L. Mencken might have made light of the squeaky-clean Shriners' mystical clubhouse on Michigan Avenue. But 60 years later, irony was on the Shriners' side: a fanciful historical conceit when it was constructed, the building had become a genuine historical treasure. Long since vacated by its builders, the charmed and cursed structure caught the attention of elite European hoteliers looking for an appropriate venue in Chicago. Inter-Continental Hotels teamed up with a local developer to make the former Shriners' club into a landmark hotel.

Name	Hotel Inter-Continental Chicago
Location	Chicago, Illinois
Owner	Inter-Continental Hotels
Operator	Inter-Continental Hotels
Type of Hotel	Luxury
Date of Original Construction	1929
Number of Rooms	887
Bars & Restaurants	2 restaurants / 1 bar
Meeting Rooms (Number & Size)	32 / 44,142 square feet
Recreation Facilities	Indoor pool, sauna, aerobics room, exsercise machines, massage area
Type of Renovation	First phase: closure for rehabilitation of public spaces, gut of guest room floors Second phase: hotel operating during renovations
Cost	$140 Million
Date	First phase: 1988 -1990 Second phase: 1993-1994
Developer (first phase)	M.A.T. Associates. Chicago
Architect	First phase: Harry Weese & Associates, Chicago Second phase: W. Steven Gross, AIA, Chicago
Interior Designer	Design Continuum, Atlanta, Georgia
Consultants	Structural Engineer: Cohen-Barreto-Marchertas
Contractor	First phase: Mellon-Stuart Co., Chicago Second phase: Walbridge-Aldinger

EXOTIC WELCOME
The main lobby of the historic Medinah Athletic Club greets guests with its original Arabic "As Selamu Aleikum" portal inscription. Before the restoration, the polychromed ceiling was almost black — and the stone walls had been painted white. The walls were stripped, the ceiling restored and a custom carpet milled to match the original one.
Photograph by John Miller © Hedrich Blessing

MIGHTY PRESENCE
Although the colors and materials are.more restrained on the exterior than on the interior, the building does betray its eclectic nature to passersby, with balconies, loggias. and Assyrian-inspired projecting windows. The dome at the top of the building was regilded and the flagpole was added as part of the renovation. The smaller tower added in the 1960s is to the left, behind the historic tower. Not the only historic building left in a modern city, the hotel is listed on the National Register of Historic Places and is part of the Michigan-Wacker Historic District, noted for its concentration of early-20th-century skyscrapers which make the building look very much at home (above).
Photographs by Hedrich Blessing

ELEVATING WALLS TO A NEW HEIGHT
The Italian Renaissance design in the elevator lobby does not stop at plaster moldings — the entire wall and ceiling surface is polychromed, and frescoes fill the arches over the elevator doors. These surfaces were intact before the renovation and were cleaned and preserved (top). A historic view (below) shows the room, seen from the adjoining Court which was lit dramatically to accent its full intrigue.
Color photograph by Ira Montgomery.

COLOR REGAINED
The columns and capitals in the Court, a circulation and pre-function space on the fourth floor, had been painted white before the renovation. The paint was stripped and the capitals were regilded. The carpet was custom-milled on a floral design inspired by the original Spanish tile wainscot on the wall in the background. The wall covering in the room seen in the background (right) through the Gothic arch was custom-designed, based on historic photographs (left) of the space.
Photograph by John Miller ©
Hedrich Blessing

Despite its impressive start, history treated the Medinah Athletic Club unkindly: it went out of business in 1934 with the Depression, ending up as a hotel in 1944. It went through stints as a Sheraton and a Radisson, and a second tower, 26 stories high with 500 rooms, was added in 1961. In 1986, the property closed, and in 1988 the restoration began. Inter-Continental Hotels purchased the property outright in 1989. The first renovation project was completed in 1990, and a second phase of work was carried out from 1993 to 1994 without closing the hotel.

The renovation required making order out of a patchwork of eras and uses, while showcasing the grandiose aspects of the original building. The renovation team decided to rehabilitate the public spaces on the first eight floors of the building, which included almost all the remaining impressive social rooms from the Medinah Athletic Club. Many of the original interior finishes, hidden as securely as Shriners' club secrets by decades of paint, carpeting and other alterations, were exposed and restored. Most spaces were faithfully returned to their original details and colors with help

from a Shriner who learned about the project and brought in a commemorative book printed at the opening of the club, complete with good photographs of the interior.

The renovation team made intentional changes in a few rooms, such as the entry, which had been a very masculine space with a Celtic theme. It was opened up and brightened considerably to welcome the public. Except for the indoor swimming pool on the fourteenth floor. the building was gutted above the eighth floor to accommodate a rational layout of new

guest rooms and systems meeting current standards. Back-of-the-house areas on the first eight floors were also gutted.

The Indiana limestone exterior of the building was cleaned and the dome, which crowns it, was gilded and fitted out with an American flag. Long-term overhauls and deferred maintenance of exterior elements proceeded through both phases of the renovation. The first round of the renovation created two hotels, the Inter-Continental in the original Medinah building and the Forum in the newer tower addition. The Forum Hotel opened in September 1989 and the Inter-Continental opened in March, 1990. Forum is a business hotel chain owned by Inter-Continental; the Chicago Forum was the firm's only location in the United States when it opened. Although operated as two

hotels, the Forum and the Inter-Continental shared management, staff, back-of-the-house areas — and clientele, as time went by. Food and beverage outlets and meeting rooms lured guests both ways between the two hotels, prompting management to fold the Forum into the Inter-Continental in November, 1993.

To consolidate the two, a new main entry lobby and registration lobby were built in

the newer (Forum) tower, the banquet rooms and guest rooms in the newer tower were renovated and a new exterior canopy was constructed at the new main entrance. The elevator cabs, public toilet rooms and back-of-the-house areas in the newer tower were also redone, and a new gift shop was constructed, allowing the existing gift shop in the historic part of the hotel to be converted into a business services center.

AERIE DINING
The Boulevard Restaurant, which overlooks the entry lobby of the historic building, gives diners not only a vantage point over comings and goings below but a close look at the historic polychromed ceiling of the lobby. Because the ceiling and column capitals are so intricate, the furniture was kept simple to keep the setting from becoming overpowering. A special dining area over the exterior entry to the lobby has a central view and a special table of inlaid wood (above).
Photographs by
Ira Montgomery.

RESTORATION DINING

The Renaissance Room was paneled in Carpathian burled elm, and lit by Baccarat chandeliers. The paneling was thoroughly cleaned and missing pieces restored to the chandeliers. The stack chairs are inspired by the musical images carved in the stone posts which terminate the iron railing along the raised seating area on the perimeter of the room (right). The brass-finished chairs, custom-designed for the renovation, were later added to the furniture manufacturer's standard line.

Photograph by Ira Montgomery

COME AROUND FULL CIRCLE
Document research and site investigations guided the renovation team to the original design of the ballroom. The carpet was custom designed from photographs of the original, the column capitals and ceiling were regilded after the white paint which had been applied in an earlier remodeling was removed, and the ceiling frescoes which ring the room between the columns were restored by the conservator.
Photographs by Hedrich Blessing

THE RAIN IN SPAIN Doesn't land in the 25 meter pool built by the Shriners, but one might think it did. The Spanish-Colonial fountain, majolica tile and coffered ceiling help create the atmosphere of a hacienda — 14 floors above Michigan Avenue.
Photograph by
Ira Montgomery

MYSTERY AND MAJESTY The Salon, a lobby lounge adjacent to the entry lobby of the historic building, echoes the eastern intrigue of the historic interiors with its Empire chairs with griffin's wing arms and loosely Persian-inspired drapes in reds and teals with gold lining.
Photograph by
Ira Montgomery

The renovation process was as complicated as the history of the building. To
minimize front-end costs and streamline
design and construction, the developer,
M.A.T. Associates, made the project fast-
track design-build. That provided a
guaranteed maximum construction cost
and a single point of responsibility for
design and construction. Design proceeded without investigations and
drawings of concealed existing elements,
and began with just schematic architectural and mechanical drawings. Then
the fun began. The original building's
structural system was significantly
different than designers had supposed.
"There were lateral (framing) elements
all over the place" requiring the designers, contractor, developer and hotel
operators to change the design every step
of the way, said architect Steve Gross,
who worked on both phases of the
renovation. "You can just imagine the
wars that arose."

The project team rolled with the
punches, even changing floor layouts to
cope with surprises when walls and
ceilings were opened, meeting constantly
on site and preparing sketches almost
daily — frequently resulting in change
orders. Even without surprises or
changes, the building would have been
complicated. Because of exterior wall
setbacks on the upper floors, there are
more than 20 different floor plans for
the guest room levels of the building.
"It's not a cookie cutter set of accommodations in any way," said Stan Allan,
chairman of Harry Weese Associates.
"The man who installed in the carpeting
wished it were".

WORSHIPFUL MASTERS, SATRAPS AND PANJANDRUMS
Suites in the renovated hotel are fit for today's rich and famous as well as the mythical royalty who inspired the public spaces in the building. Each suite has its own design and color scheme. The one at the top of the building has a two story living room, dining area, master bedroom, guest bedroom, and two bathrooms.
Photographs by Ira Montgomery.

Guest rooms feature built-in mini bar; clock radio, voice mail; telephone and hair dryer in the bathroom; and remote color television which can display messages and the guest's bill, and call the bell captain. Furniture is Empire, chosen for the guest rooms and many of the public spaces because it repeats some of the visual themes found in the eclectic period references of the historic public spaces. Rooms in the historic part of the building were small before the renovation, but the gutting of guest room floors meant that room sizes could be increased and the room count lowered.

The renovation updated the health facilities from the mystical-men's club image of the 1920s to the fitness-on-the-go and relaxation requirements of 1990s hotel guests. Facilities, originally spread over many stories, were consolidated on three levels around the original swimming pool on the fourteenth floor. The pool was restored to its 1920s exotic splendor, while the adjoining new facilities on the twelfth and thirteenth floors include a weight room with Paramount exercise equipment and free weights, an aerobics room with a suspended flooring system, and a cardiovascular room with four Lifecycles, two treadmills, and two Lifestep machines. Each changing room has a sauna and there is a massage area.

THEN AND NOW
A historic view of the ballroom (right) and a view taken after renovation (above) show the original wall covering and the one designed for the restoration from the photograph of the original. The stairway to the upper level gallery in the color photograph is new.
Color photograph by
Ira Montgomery.

NO HOTEL GENERIC
Guest room floors, completely gutted in the renovation, do not have the full eccentric eclecticism of the public spaces, but they were designed to complement the original building. Furniture in the guest rooms continues the Empire theme of public spaces, but in a looser interpretation. Carpet is an Axminster custom design. Drapes are a French toile with dark green dust ruffles and border. The furniture is a mix of woods and finishes. There are two color schemes: red and forest green.

Photograph by Ira Montgomery

Omni Severin Hotel
Indianapolis, Indiana

When Mansur Development Corporation
bought the Atkinson Hotel in 1988, it had
all the ingredients for a historic hotel
rebirth in a city center bouncing back
from urban decline - and also a lot of the
hallmarks of a failed property destined for
a date with a wrecking crew. Located
across the street from a new "festival
marketplace," one block from the Indiana
Convention Center and Hoosier Dome
complex, it was a venerable pre-World War
II grande dame. But it had been closed by
its previous owner, leaving years of
deferred maintenance on top of a
mish-mash of renovations which made it
outmoded, not timeless.

ORIGINAL ELEGANCE
*The historic hotel lobby no longer functions as the main entrance or
registration area, but its restoration offers guests a space with historic
prestige. Some features of the original lobby, such as the blue ceiling, red
and blue upholstery and furniture style, were repeated in the new lobby.*

Name	**Omni Severin Hotel**
Location	**Indianapolis, Indiana**
Owner	**Mansur Development Corp.**
Operator	**Omni Hotels, Hampton, N.H.**
Type of Hotel	**Luxury**
Date of Original Construction	**1913**
Number of Rooms	**423**
Meeting Rooms (Number & Size)	**17 / 16,000 Square feet**
Bars & Restaurants	**Severin Bar & Grill, Caffeet**
Recreation Facilities	**Health club with indoor pool and exercise facilities**
Type of Renovation	**Renovation and addition; hotel shut down during construction**
Cost	**$40 Million**
Date	**Completed January 1990**
Architect	**Ratio Architects, Inc., Indianapolis**
Interior Designer	**J.P. Courteaud, New York, N.Y.**
Consultants	**Structural engineer, addition: Gunnin Campbell, Dallas, TX Structural engineer, existing building: MTA, Indianapolis**
Contractor	**F. A. Wilhemn Construction Co., Inc.**

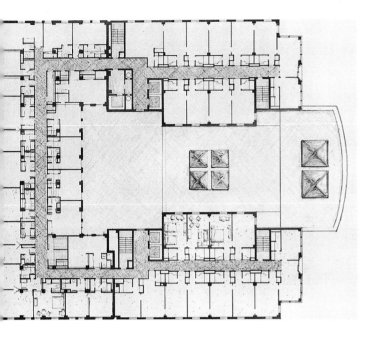

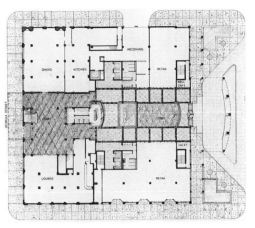

NATURAL GROWTH

On the ground floor, the lobby of the addition (plan above: green area at right with burgundy zone inside it) terminates in the new registration desk, which abuts the lobby of the original building (burgundy area at left). The motor entrance of the new lobby (far right) faces the city's rehabilitated train station. Upper floor corridors in the original hotel (C-shaped portion of building in plan at left) flow naturally into the corridors of the two wings of the addition (horizontal extensions to the right on top and bottom of drawing). Elevators and stairs are all located in new portion of the building.

NEW INTRODUCTION

The new hotel lobby, located at the center of the addition, is two stories high and has a large skylight to increase the sense of openness offered by the glass wall facing the Indianapolis Union Station festival marketplace across the street. Glass railings and the sleek fountain help reinforce the contemporary character which strongly distinguishes the addition from the historic hotel, but traditional furniture and marble which matches that in the original building serve to tie the two parts of the renovated hotel together.

Confronted by so many opportunities and problems, Mansur decided to tackle them all at once. It doubled the size of the building with an addition offering new facilities and a new look, and renovated the old part of the building to capitalize on its history. To make the most of the recently rehabilitated Union Station festival marketplace across the street from the expansion site adjacent to the original hotel, Mansur and the designer, Ratio Architects placed the main entrance and lobby of the reno-vated property in the addition. The addition, although carefully tailored to complement the massing, layout, design and materials of the original building, is decidedly modern, announcing strongly that the hotel is not what it used to be. Along with the new lobby, the addition contains a health club and swimming pool, retail and meeting spaces, new guest rooms, and two-level suites on its top floor.

In plan, the addition transforms the nearly rectangular original hotel into a U-shaped layout. On upper floors, the center of the U is an open courtyard, while on the ground floor it is occupied by the new lobby. Floor levels in the addition match those in the existing building, and corridors on upper floors of the addition connect to those of the original building. There were seven different guest room sizes before the renovation, with most of them small, according to Mansur President Cornelius M. Alig. The smallest rooms were combined, and rooms in the addition were sized generously, with special suite-sized rooms on the end of each wing, boasting floor-to-ceiling windows on three sides and balconies overlooking Union Station across the street. The two-story suites which top off the addition have proven popular as hospi-tality suites and for executive and luxury travel.

OLD COLONY CLUB

HOTEL SEVERIN
Indianapolis, Ind.

EARLY DAYS
Postcards from the 1920s show the historic Hotel Severin in its young glory.
Lobby is at lower right; photos on left and at upper right show the Old
Colony Club, an original lounge on the mezzanine overlooking the lobby

NEW EXPOSURE

The inner courtyard and south end of the addition (foreground) are clad in concrete and glass to strengthen the building's contemporary identity, while the sides of the addition (left side) are mostly brick, which blends with the old part of the building (at rear on left side). Paired window openings on the sides of the addition mimic the design of the historic building. The architects designed the concrete-framed balconies of the two-story suites at the top of the addition to avoid a visual conflict with the elaborate cornice of the original building, and chose green-tinted glass to mirror the color of patina of exposed copper elements on the old building.

COMPLEMENTARY DESIGN

The addition (at rear) takes its cues from the historic hotel (in front of drawing right) in order to blend in with it instead of overwhelming it. Floor levels are the same, roof lines match, and the brick and concrete of the addition are the counterparts of the brick and limestone of the historic hotel. The arched windows on the ground floor of the historic building had been closed for years before the renovation and were brought back to recreate the exterior. The entrance marquise was retained, but cars and taxies no longer line up as they did 50 years ago (left), because the main entrance to the hotel is now in the addition, on the opposite side of the building.

BLEND OF TASTES
The restaurant of the renovated hotel is located in the new section of the building, and while it has a contemporary tone, features such as furniture and lighting suggest the style of the original part of the property.

BRINGING BACK OLD MEMORIES
Although the Severin Ballroom in the historic part of the hotel had never been eliminated, its windows had been filled with concrete masonry. This was removed during the renovation so the windows could be restored. The original walnut and mahogany paneling had been covered with paint decades ago which could not be removed because of cost and logistical problems, but the vaulted plaster ceilings and egg-and-dart molding were restored during the renovation.

On the interior, as on the exterior, the addition was intended to look boldly new, not like an clone of the historic hotel. Although some of the furniture is traditional, much is sharply modern. Indiana-based Kimball International designed and supplied new furniture intended to complement the antiques the hotel had acquired during an earlier renovation in the 1960s. In the original hotel, important spaces such as the lobby were brought back to their historic condition. Its molded plaster detailing and monumental marble staircase were restored, and the cast iron railing of the lobby mezzanine, removed years earlier when the mezzanine was covered over, was restored and reinstalled.

The renovation included all-new mechanical, electrical, plumbing and life safety systems for the existing building. The main kitchen was remodeled, hotel offices were moved to space in the basement formerly occupied by the coffee shop, and the elevators and one stairway were removed to make room for a service area and additional guest room on each floor. Stairs and elevators serving the whole building are located in the addition.

BIGGER AND BRIGHTER
On the ends of the two guest room wings which make up the upper floors of the addition are extra-large rooms with a sitting area and a bed area. These rooms have balconies and floor-to-ceiling glass on three sides. The color schemes for guest rooms are based on rich burgundies, teals and browns.

SIXTIES LOOK
A remodel of the original hotel in the 1960s gave the building a "contemporary" look of that time, with suspended metal-grid ceilings, flush doors and wall paneling with minimal trim and moldings.

The Pfister Hotel
Milwaukee, Wisconsin

When the Pfister Hotel in Milwaukee went bankrupt and was in danger of demolition thirty years ago, local businessman Ben Marcus led a group of investors who rescued it by adding a tower with parking garage, meeting facilities and a swimming pool completed in 1966.

The 23-story tower also renovated for the first time as part of the project, still provides half the convention floor, a parking garage, recreation facilities, and a rooftop nightclub and other amenities, often missing in 19th-century hotels, but the older part of the building assures the property its image as the authentic venue for Milwaukee's establishment. Architectural features which were covered for decades have been exposed, original materials renewed and historic spaces reconstituted.

Name	**The Pfister Hotel**
Location	**Milwaukee, Wisconsin**
Owner	**The Marcus Corporation**
Operator	**Marcus Hotels and Resorts**
Type of Hotel	**Luxury**
Date of Original Construction	**1893**
Number of Rooms	**307**
Bars & Restaurants	**The English Room**
	Lobby Lounge
	Cafe at the Pfister
	Cafe Rouge
	La Playa Lounge
Meeting Rooms (Number & Size)	**8 / 24,000 square feet**
Recreation Facilities	**Swimming pool, exercise machines**
Type of Renovation	**Phased, hotel open throughout**
Cost	**Not disclosed officially**
Date	**1988 - 1993**
Architect	**Schroeder and Holt Architects, Inc., Waukesha, Wisconsin**
Interior Designer	**First phase: O'Hara & Associates, Oak Brook, Illinois**
	Second phase: Hirsch/Bedner Associates, Los Angeles, California
Consultants	**Structural Engineer: Strass-Maguire & Associates, Milwaukee, Wisconsin**
Contractor	**Tri-North Builders, Madison, Wisconsin**
	Thomas & Egenhoefer, Inc., Menomonee Falls, Wisconsin
	Hunzinger Construction Co., Brookfield, Wisconsin

Hotel Pfister, Milwaukee, Wis.

ODD COUPLE
When the original hotel went bankrupt and was in danger of demolition thirty years ago, a modern addition and tower gave it the atmosphere and amenities it needed to survive in the market. Current photographs (below) literally turn the relationship around 180 degrees, showcasing the original building which has not changed much since it was new.
Photographs courtesy of The Pfister Hotel.

Guido Pfister, a German immigrant who made a fortune in the tannery in Milwaukee, envisioned the hotel and bought the land where it stands, but died before its construction. His son, Charles, and daughter, Louise, took over the project and supervised the opening in 1893. Milwaukee was a leading U.S. industrial center at the time, and the $1.5 million hotel aimed to surpass the luxury lodgings any city could offer. Outside, a monumental Romanesque Revival stone structure emphasized solidity and tradition, while inside, there was a pharmacy, separate billiards rooms and lounges for men and women, a ladies' music room, and a Turkish bath.

The hotel featured a two-story lobby with a barrel-vaulted skylighted glass ceiling, bordered by a grand open iron staircase. The ornate detailing of the capitals on the marble columns, the nearly continuous wall moldings, the upper floor railings and balustrades, and the light fixtures were typical of late-19th-century architecture, as was the industrial appearance of the glazed ceiling, creating an overall impression of a grandiose reflection of the past, made possible by an industrial boom. The skylighted glass ceiling was removed in 1926, when the hotel underwent its first renovation. Over the years, other changes occurred, obscuring original features and cutting up important spaces, such as the lobby. When Marcus rescued the bankrupt hotel, the emphasis was on competing with newer hotels by adding required facilities in the tower.

CENTENNIAL SPACE
The lobby of the original Pfister Hotel building at the turn of the century impressed Milwau-kee with its opulence (facing page), and after a complete refurbishment and restoration of some of its long-concealed historic features, it helped keep the property in the limelight in 1993 (main view below, after renovation). The glass ceiling in the original lobby had been removed decades ago; instead of reconstructing it, designers added a painted sky in the vault, complete with renaissance cherubs.
Photographs courtesy of The Pfister Hotel.

When the centenary of the hotel approached, Marcus and his son Stephen, chief executive of the family hotel operation, vowed to restore the original building for the occasion. The centerpiece of the project became reclamation and refurbishment of the lobby and original features, rounded out by overhauls of restaurants. The room count was reduced from 333 to 307, and all-new systems were installed in the original building. Phased construction allowed the hotel to remain in operation during the renovation. The first phase covered guest rooms in the original building, and the second phase refurbished the remainder of the original hotel and most of the 1960s addition.

The hotel's historic lobby did not regain its skylighted glass ceiling, but a painted sky mural in the same barrel vault shape was introduced in its place. Unsympathetic changes in finishes made over the years, such as a contrasting dark and light paint scheme on molding panels and velour wallpaper applied over scagliola columns, were removed and the original materials restored. To restore the original scale of the lobby, a café-lounge which had been inserted by partitioning off one side of the space was removed, and the outside entry vestibule, not original to the building, was halved in depth.

The removal of a light-fare restaurant which had been within the historic lobby revealed a historic fireplace, mantel and ornamental chimney hood which had been shrouded by Spanish-themed paneling. When the lobby was restored to its original size, the original fireplace and surround and the imported marble flooring around the fireplace were exposed and restored. The restored space has been renamed the Lobby Lounge, and offers drinks and light meals throughout the day.

The other restaurants and bars in the hotel were not reconfigured, although all but one were updated. The English Room, the hotel's fine dining restaurant, had been altered over the decades, with the addition of discordant touches such as a bright blue acoustic tile ceiling. A major overhaul restored its original image with stained wood paneling, upholstered wall covering and a coffered ceiling with custom chandeliers. The bar, once a completely separate space, was united visually with the dining area.

HISTORIC DISCOVERY
The removal of a light-fare restaurant which had been partitioned out of space in the historic lobby revealed a historic fireplace, mantel, and ornamental chimney hood which had been shrouded by Spanish-themed paneling. The fireplace was the centerpiece of the seating area of the lobby decades ago (above) and has regained that role, with comfortable couches and back tables and lamps (bottom).
Photographs courtesy of
The Pfister Hotel.

The former Greenery coffee shop, with white booths, green and white wall covering and mirrored columns, was recast as the Café at the Pfister, with more of a bistro flavor. Natural wood gives it a warmer and richer feeling, and an archway was added to articulate better the transition between the two dining areas. The Cafe Rouge, the main restaurant in the original part of the hotel, was renovated along with the guest rooms in that building. Having suffered few changes over the years, its design stayed relatively stable during the restoration, with new finishes that elaborated the original theme. La Playa Lounge, a nightclub atop the tower which overlooks the Milwaukee skyline and Lake Michigan, had been renovated in the early 1980s; management delayed further renovation until after the main project was complete.

The renovation updated the meeting rooms, although it did not include major changes in layout. In the main space in

the original building, the Imperial Ballroom the historic coffered ceiling was repainted and accented with hand-applied gold leaf and faux marble. New recessed downlights help the historic chandeliers meet contemporary lighting requirements. A new conference room was added on the second floor, and combined with an adjacent guest bedroom, it can also serve as a suite.

In the original building, guest room floor corridors and exterior walls did not change, but everything between them was gutted. Because the distance between the corridors and the exterior walls varies in different parts of each floor, the new guest rooms were laid out in three sizes: single, mini-suite (bedroom with a parlor area) and full suite (bedroom and separate parlor). The bathrooms, which had raised floors before the renovation because of constraints in installing plumbing in the 1893 construction, were rebuilt at the same floor level as the bedrooms. Al-

though the layout of guest room floors in the tower did not change, the look was altered radically. The typical 1960s contemporary tone of the rooms and the cool gray color schemes contrasted too much with the original building. The renovation used transitional furniture including Chinese Chippendale, and Renaissance Revival, 1930s club chairs and Empire mirrors. and soft gold wall coverings to warm the rooms and relate them to the rest of the hotel. Draperies with valences and side panels and case pieces with exotic veneers help soften the rooms. The round footprint of the tower creates novel geometries in guest rooms and public spaces; floral carpeting in hallways deemphasizes the curved walls.

OLD FAVORITE
The existing red and white color scheme of the Café Rouge, which serves brunch and a luncheon buffet, was elaborated with application of contrasting colors to ceiling moldings and faux-marble paint to the columns.
Photographs courtesy of The Pfister Hotel.

HISTORY RENEWED
The Imperial Ballroom boasted a historic interior which was well preserved and did not call out for a drastic makeover. The designers made subtle moves, such as adding new drapery rich in swags, jabots, tassels and trim and restoring the ceiling.
Photographs courtesy of The Pfister Hotel.

STAYING WITH TRADITION

Guest rooms in the original part of the building (right) let the property's venerable history shine through, even though everything in them is new. Deluxe rooms feature four-poster beds, while others have pediment headboards. All have traditional furniture in mahogany, brass lamps and warm color schemes. Although the new rooms look traditional, they are far from an exact replica of the hotel's past, judging by a hotel archive view of a guest room in the 1920s. Furniture in renovated rooms in the 1960s tower (bottom) has a traditional feeling, and colors are warm and rich to strengthen the association with the original building. Generous drapes with side panels help reduce the impact of the curved exterior walls of the building.

Photographs courtesy of The Pfister Hotel.

The renovation also included installation of firesprinklers throughout the property, major upgrades in back-of-the-house areas, including kitchen and the employee cafeteria, and alterations to comply with the Americans with Disabilities Act. The mechanical, electrical, plumbing and alarm systems in the original building were replaced. The 1960s tower was renovated several floors at a time, and remained open while the original portion of the building was closed.

One part of the hotel the owner avoided changing is the art collection. Art in the hotel includes 80 original oil and water-color paintings from the collection of Charles Pfister. The hotel says this is the largest collection of 19-century art held by any hotel in the world. It is still on display, from watercolors and oil paintings in the corridors to bronze lions in the lobby.

MARBLE AND MIRRORS
Renovated bathrooms are a big change, especially in the original part of the building, which opened in 1893 with 200 private rooms—and only 61 private bathrooms. The renovated hotel has a totally new plumbing system, and a private bath in each room. This suite bath has a slick look with mirrored walls, whirlpool tub, and marble flooring and tub surround in contrasting colors. Wicker furniture complements the luxury theme while softening the feeling of the other materials.
Photographs courtesy of The Pfister Hotel.

The Wigwam Resort
Litchfield Park, Arizona

The Southwestern style would be the natural choice of any owner, operator or designer for renovating the Wigwam Resort in Litchfield Park, Ariz., but that does not mean everyone would work it the same way. Now more than 75 years old, the sprawling adobe-covered resort with three golf courses and lush gardens had already been renovated in the Southwestern style about 20 years before designer Jill Cole of Cole Martinez Curtis and Associates took it on. There were many practical and measurable criteria for the current renovation, including: improve functionality, build more *casita* guest rooms, add meeting space, and reorganize the food and beverage outlets. But primary was a less tangible goal: retain the resort's Five Diamond/Four Star rating from the Mobil and American Automobile Association guides, and keep the property firmly established as a luxury resort. Beyond obvious formulas, that means giving a property style. And for the Wigwam, the question was not which style to choose, but how to interpret the Southwestern style.

TERRITORIAL IMPERATIVE
Rustic, informal Territorial style is the real thing, not an affectation, at the Wigwam. This historic photograph shows the main lodge before golf carts —or automobiles — were the favored mode of transportation.

Name	The Wigwam Resort and Country Club
Location	Litchfield Park, Arizona
Owner	Kabuto International, San Francisco
Operator	Suncor Development Company
Type of Hotel	Luxury Resort/Conference
Date of Original Construction	Built 1919, Hotel opened 1929
Number of Rooms	331
Bars & Restaurants	Arizona Bar, Kachina Lounge, Terrace Dining Room, Arizona Kitchen
Meeting Rooms (Number & Size)	16 / 26,000 square feet
Recreation Facilities	Pool, spa, three 18-hole golf courses, nine tennis courts.
Type of Renovation	Phased, renovation construction during annual summer closing
Cost	$28 million
Date	1987-1991
Architect	Allen & Philp Architects, Inc. (main building) Scottsdale, Ariz. Shepherd, Nelson & Wheeler (tennis casitas), Phoenix, Ariz.
Interior Designer	Cole Martinez Curtis and Associates, Marina del Rey, Calif.
Contractor	Kitchell Contractors, Inc., Phoenix, Ariz.

HOME AT HEART
The Fireplace Lounge, originally the registration lobby, evokes the origins of the property as a homey private lodge for the Goodyear Tire and Rubber Company. The 1919 adobe fireplace is original; doors and windows with the Indian "god's eye" motif are custom replicas of originals.
Photograph by Toshi Yoshimi.

ALL THAT GLITTERS
Is not gold in the renovated Kachina Lounge, named for
the images of Indian dolls the hotel had in its art
collection. The centerpiece of the space, where guests
can order drinks and look out over the patio, is a new
custom-designed river rock bar topped with a shiny
hammered copper bar.
Photographs by Toshi Yoshimi.

TAKING CARE OF BUSINESS
Although the resort is primarily a vacation destination, it also offers meeting and conference facilities, which were expanded in the renovation. The Palm Room (top) offers a boardroom setting, while the Sachem Hall (left) functions as a large meeting room or ballroom. Meeting rooms all have new ceilings, new sound systems and new lighting.
Photographs by Toshi Yoshimi.

The hotel is a product of that style, and an authentic example of it. Built in 1919 as the "Organization House" for Goodyear Tire and Rubber Company operations nearby, it started out as a single lodge with adobe exterior walls, opened to the public in 1929 with 13 guest rooms and grew over the next 30 years as *casitas* (small freestanding buildings with guest rooms), a country club, and a swimming pool were added. Additional buildings were later sprinkled throughout the gardens which grew up around the original lodge. The lodge now houses public spaces, meeting rooms and back-of-the-house areas only. As the property matured, so did appreciation for Arizona's early heritage, making Southwestern or Territorial style central to the product offered to guests. When Suncor Development Company, a subsidiary of Pinnacle West Capital Corporation, bought the 463-acre resort in 1986, its latest renovation was decades old and the luxury label was in jeopardy. The new owner launched a near-total renovation, which was followed by major expansion of guest and meeting rooms.

SOMETHING NEW UNDER THE SUN
The Sun Lounge (facing page), located near the registration lobby and the path to the major lounges and food and beverage outlets, is rustic and intimate with informal seating groups in a variety of materials and colors. Elegant Indian-inspired artifacts and a reupholstered original bench on new green slate flooring with cozy-rugs, complement the original entry's ashlar slate steps (above). The new doors to the patio incorporate the God's eye motif. The lamps on the far wall are cowbell wall sconces, a design original to the hotel, almost the only element that can be found in the space before and after the renovation.
Photographs by Toshi Yoshimi.

TOTALLY WIRED
The existing vernacular "beanpot" chandeliers embody the informal and indigenous character of the Wigwam, but they did not pass muster with the electrical code. Instead of discarding them, the renovation team rewired them and had them certified for reinstallation by Underwriters' Laboratories — then replicated them for use in additional spaces.
Photograph by Toshi Yoshimi.

The renovation consisted of two phases: $8 million for refurbishing part of the public spaces during the annual summer shutdown of the property in 1987, and $20 million for redoing the rest of the property over an 11 month period ending in September 1988, followed by the expansion of the meeting rooms. By the time the project was completed, the renovation team had redesigned 175 guest rooms, built 22 new *casita* rooms around the tennis courts, and reworked the dining, entertainment and conference facilities in the main lodge. Following the renovation, three new two-story buildings with 90 deluxe guest rooms of 540 square feet each, and a new 11,000 square foot ballroom were completed in November 1991.

The previous renovation reflected "contemporary" design of the 1960s as much as it did the Territorial Style of pre-statehood Arizona which shaped the original lodge . Traditional decorative motifs were used — but abstracted into clean, crisp forms; geometric patterns showed up in carpets, but regularized in a way that suggested the Machine Age as much as the pueblo; and products like fluorescent lighting, mirrored walls and plastic laminates popped up left and right. Only an exact historic restoration would be utterly free of contemporary aesthetics, Cole admitted, and the renovation completed in 1990 is far from that. While taking into account requirements for the property's rating and guest expectations, "as much as possible, we tried to be as genuine as we could," said Cole. "Of course, we didn't put spittoons in the corners."

To tint the building in a contemporary light and make it meet current market needs without diminishing its historical essence, the designers used indigenous and traditional materials such as leathers, cottons and river rock. They found a local blacksmith to make wrought iron door hardware and selected woods similar to those found locally in 1919, which are no longer available.

Photographs guided the designers in returning spaces to their original condition or casting new elements in the spirit of the old, but some research pointed in a direction that was not so easy to follow. Although the photographs are black and white, Cole knew that the colors used in the 1920s were from Indian blankets. The traditional Indian colors, gray, black and brown, made a palette that was too dull and brown for contemporary hotel guests, so the design team reached out to the surrounding countryside for inspiration. The result is a blend of desert-jewel tones and earthy colors: lavender, turquoise, sand, green rose, terra cotta, pink, adobe and cinnamon. "The color palette is utterly artistic license," Cole said.

UPPER CRUST
The renovation added a new fine dining restaurant, the Arizona Kitchen. Its simple, spare design helps draw attention to the dramatically-lighted open kitchen; the brick floor, stucco walls and wooden ceiling add softness and a rustic feeling to the 100-seat space.
Photograph by Toshi Yoshimi.

SMALLER PORTIONS

Servings are the same size, but the main dining room, which had been one large room seating 300, was broken into three so that small numbers of diners would not feel they were eating in an abandoned warehouse. Antler-motif chandeliers and wall sconces, a stylized traditional viga and latilla ceiling, adobe walls, and stained glass windows with the God's eye motif make reference to the original hotel's traditional style. Before the renovation (left), the single dining room had large-pane windows with modern window treatment, extensive downlighting and acoustic tile on the ceiling.

Photographs by Toshi Yoshimi.

WINTER WARMTH
The new casitas surrounding the tennis courts have large living areas with fireplaces and separate bedrooms. Wood shutters with adjustable louvers in the living room add to the bright and informal feeling while emphasizing the prestige of the property.
Photographs by Toshi Yoshimi.

MORE OF A GOOD THING
To help the property eliminate its traditional annual closing during Arizona's scorching summers, the existing pool was expanded and shade structures were added (background) to supplement umbrellas. The firepit in the foreground (bottom) was added to take advantage of summer nights when the desert is pleasantly cool.
Photographs by Toshi Yoshimi.

NO PUTTING INDOORS, PLEASE

Guests don't have to be told not to practice putting in their rooms when they stay in the Fairway Casa guest rooms, which open directly onto the golf course. There are two guest room color schemes, based on the bedspread: blue (shown here), accented by terra cotta, green and cinnamon and adobe, complemented by turquoise, lavender and orange. Typical guest rooms, as well as suites, have a wet bar and eating area (top). Bathrooms have been improved from plastic laminate counters and stock tile before the renovation (bottom) to countertops and floors in a matching tile designed to replicate the soft handmade tile typical of early Southwestern building.
Photographs by Toshi Yoshimi.

There were tremendous variations amongst the guest rooms, and some bizarre features. This was good news, because it added interest and authenticity, but bad news because it created the impression that some rooms were inferior to others in the same grade. Designers tried to standardize the rooms without sterilizing them. The renovation included consistent features such as patios, minibars, separate living and sleeping areas and safes, while retaining the individuality of each room.

Although the renovated hotel looks very up-.to-date, Cole would not mind if guests think otherwise. "We wanted even the new construction to look as if it could have been built in the '20s," she said.

Arizona Biltmore
Phoenix, Arizona

The Arizona Biltmore in Phoenix seemed to have a lot going for it in 1991: a historic building with the signature of America's greatest architect, a developed 39-acre site, and a climate that has been drawing guests from thousands of miles away for a century. What change did the owners want when they began a four-year phased renovation? The best answer is "More of the same."

The $33 million renovation aimed to reinforce the luxury status of the property and add to its historic luster. In addition to renovating guest rooms and public spaces, it adds to existing amenities, including doubling the swimming pools and adding a water slide and new cabanas. A new 16,000 square foot flexible ballroom, 76 new luxury villas built for sale, and a new 18-hole putting course headed the list of additions.

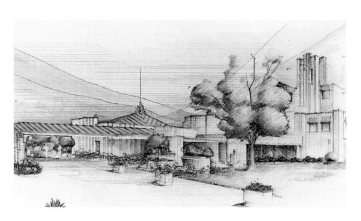

MADE IN THE SHADE
Although the renovation did not make drastic changes to the lobby, it did add a new entry and porte cochere to improve guests' first impressions. The addition keeps guests dry the few days it rains each year, and provides a respite from the Arizona sun which beats down the rest of the time.

Name	Arizona Biltmore
Location	Phoenix, Arizona
Owner	Biltmore Hotel Properties
Operator	Grossmann Properties Co.
Type of Hotel	Resort / Luxury
Date of Original Construction	1929
Number of Rooms	498
Bars & Restaurants	5 restaurants / 1 bar
Meeting Rooms (Number & Size)	19 rooms / 39,000 square feet
Recreation Facilities	4 pools, 92-foot water slide, "Kids' Kabana," 2 18-hole golf courses, 18-hole putting course, lawn games, 8 tennis courts, jogging/hiking trails, fitness center and spa
Type of Renovation	Phased renovation, hotel open during most work
Cost	$33 million
Date	1991-1995 (Projected)
Architect	Vernon Swaback Associates, Scottsdale, Arizona
Interior Designer	Barry Design Associates, Los Angeles, California
Contractor	D.L.Withers Construction, Inc.

Although the renovation included new finishes and interior design for public areas, it stressed maintaining the appearance which had made the hotel famous since Albert Chase McArthur designed it in 1929 with the collaboration of Frank Lloyd Wright. Changes in the recreation areas added new facilities, but were intended to "make it look older, not newer," according to W. Matthew Crow, president of the Arizona Biltmore.

In the historic lobby, there was more restoration than renovation. Carpeting was replaced with oak flooring with inset carpeted areas, while the Mission and Gustave Stickley-style furniture was reupholstered in a new color scheme more in keeping with the original design and desert setting. New lighting reduced glare by using a translucent glass version of the "Biltmore Block" custom-detailed exterior masonry units unique to the original hotel. The adjoining Lobby Lounge restaurant was opened to the canvas-covered Arizona Room on the exterior by replacing a bank of windows with doors.

Guest rooms retained their original number and layout. Half were redone in 1993 and the other half in 1994. The renovation did not change room and bathroom partitions, but all furniture, fixtures, finishes and soft goods were replaced. The renovated guest rooms reflect both the hotel's origins as a resort destination and its present situation in a major metropolis.

DESERT OASIS
The Arizona Biltmore has long drawn on vacationers from northern states who wanted to escape winter. The new pool and water slide (center, rear) enlarge the hotel's desert oasis, allowing guests who want to be surrounded by water to see the desert from a distance.

IMPROVING ON THE PAST
To enhance the Arizona Biltmore's luxury image, the architects studied the facades of some of its less prominent wings, which were originally lacking in ornamentation. The design shown for the Paradise Wing adds landscaping and horizontal detailing to the building to enliven it and break up the visual mass. The design was first applied to another wing of the hotel and then executed in additional locations.

POOLSIDE HIDEAWAY
Guests who want to stake out their own territory beside the property's new swimming pools can rent a tent-like canvas cabana, or go for the full luxury of a "standard" cabana built of masonry Biltmore Block (pictured here). The standard cabana includes a sitting area, wet bar, bathroom with shower and an outdoor sitting area by the pool with a canvas awning.

DESERT MIRAGE
Appearing for only about eight months, the Wrigley Lawn Pavilion was the renovation designers' answer to the demand for immediate expansion of meeting space. The fabric-roofed ballroom also served as a test market for flexible "new era" permanent ballroom which later replaced it on the same site.

PORTAL OF CHANGE
When converting an underutilized lawn into two new pools, the architects strived to integrate them into the existing site. This new entry gate structure incorporates the gate to the new pools with a shaded pool deck area, while using the architectural style and materials of the original building to fit the new into the old harmoniously.

Restraint is the last thing the renovation designers aimed to impose on guests at the pool area, where two new pools were added to the original two. The renovation also provided a water slide for those who want to do more than swim laps. The slide is hidden in a tower which looks more like a Wright folly than modern recreation equipment. The cabanas which surrounded the original Catalina pool were replaced with 25 new cabanas, ranging from canvas tents to masonry structures to two multi-room "hospitality cabanas." Another, called Kids' Kabana, is painted in primary colors and has games, a reading area and computers to keep young swimmers happily occupied after they're too waterlogged to stay in the pool.

In addition to resort amenities, the renovation added necessities sought by guests, including a new business center, with fax, cellular phones, pagers, printers, personal computers, lap tops and personal digital assistants. The phasing of construction allowed the Biltmore to provide three new kitchens without interrupting food service. A new kitchen serves meeting rooms, the main kitchen received an all-new interior, and a separate new kitchen gives the property Kosher food service. Other infrastructure changes included a new telephone system with voice mail and a new computer linked to electronic guest room locks and security apparatus. Guests can check in by mail, arriving at the property with pre-activated card keys, and check out using the televisions in their rooms.

The renovation also included construction of an unusual temporary meeting space on the location of an existing outdoor function area. Opened in September, 1993, the Wrigley Lawn Pavilion had a carpeted concrete foundation, fixed walls accented with replicas of "Biltmore Block," a state-of-the-art audio-visual system — and a tent-like fabric roof. A plain shell in which occupants supplied their own finished decor, it remained standing less than a year, but set the stage for the new permanent ballroom which replaced it on the same foundation. With subdued walls and a ceiling composed simply of a six-foot-square theatrical rigging grid with three-foot canvas curtains, all in black, the permanent ballroom lets users add whatever lighting and decoration they choose, or hire the hotel's events organizers to do so.

REFINING A CLASSIC
Oversized chairs with rattan detailing set a vacation tone in the renovated guest rooms, while Wright-inspired lamps and tables complement the architecture of the building. Balancing the historic and resort feeling, most fabrics and colors are muted desert tones, with standout Southwestern accents, leaving an overall impression of urbanity and restraint.

SLIDE WRIGHT IN
At first glance, guests new to the property might think this tower is part of the original hotel conceived by Frank Lloyd Wright, but
it was actually added during the renovation. The designers executed the tower in the same style as the hotel, using the concrete
"Biltmore Block" masonry at the tops and corners of the walls.

The ANA Hotel
San Francisco, California

Every city has buildings some people seem to love to hate, and hotels are just as eligible as office towers, government buildings and stores. In San Francisco, three hotels have been fixtures on the unofficial unpopularity list in recent decades, but that notoriety did not keep the ANA chain, the arm of Japan's second largest airline (Nippon Airways), from buying one of them as its first U.S. property. The ANA chain bought the former San Francisco Le Meridien, a 36-story property well-located between the Financial District and the Moscone Convention Center, and made a calculated effort to increase its architectural standing.

Name	*The ANA Hotel San Francisco*
Location	*San Francisco, California*
Owner	*ANA Hotels San Francisco, Inc.*
Operator	*ANA Enterprises, Ltd.*
Type of Hotel	*Business / Groups*
Date of Original Construction	*1983*
Number of Rooms	*673*
Bars & Restaurants	*Café Fifty Three Restaurant Lobby Bar and Lounge*
Meeting Rooms (Number & Size)	*15 / 21,000 square feet*
Recreation Facilities	*Fitness Center with exercise machines, sauna and steam room, massage*
Type of Renovation	*Reconfigure ground floor public areas, new finishes, furniture and equipment throughout. Hotel open throughout renovation.*
Cost	*$3.5 million*
Date Completed	*1993*
Architect	*The Callison Partnership, Seattle, Washington*
Interior Designer	*Barry Design Associates, Los Angeles, California*
Consultants	*Graphics: Jacquelyn Barry Structural Engineer: Structural Design Engineers, San Francisco, California Mechanical Engineer: W.L.Thompson Consulting Engineers, Atlanta, Georgia*
Contractor	*Kajima, Inc.*

REORIENTATION
The renovated spaces are articulated individually, with a more conventional and identifiable organization. The registration area focuses on a deco-inspired table accented by a three-color marble floor pattern and circular ceiling cove. The grand circulated spaces culminate with axis from the lobby to the restaurant.
Photographs by John Sutton.

Less than ten years old, the building did not have outmoded systems, decades of dinginess or giant gaps in the range of facilities demanded by the current market. Its major problem was an architectural style that detractors derided as low-budget brutalism, with a concrete exterior lacking design features other than subtle variations in color. Critics said the interior had the cold sparseness of the International Style without its strength and precision. Rather than redoing the massive exterior, ANA and its designers decided to redesign the entry and ground floor and give the interior an all new look. They chose a loose synthesis of the Art Deco and Moderne styles, thus avoiding the time warp that guests would have experienced entering an older traditional interior after approaching the relentlessly industrial facades.

The renovation made the greatest changes to the ground floor, where ANA wanted to change the original open, flowing spaces which sometimes confused guests when they tried to find their way from the entry to the registration desk. The new ground floor defines each space and organizes them around grand circulation spaces, such as a gold-domed rotunda.

A fine dining restaurant, already closed before the renovation began, was replaced with a lobby for group check-in. Offsetting the reduction in dining space, the hotel took over an adjacent alley, landscaped it and built an outdoor seating area adjacent to the restaurant and bar. Nearby, a new exterior pavilion allows the property to vie for a customary Japanese hotel market segment: weddings. The food and beverage outlets maintain a rich, masculine approach, but avoid stuffiness with bold and playful elements such as the playing-card theme which runs through from the art on the walls to the name of the restaurant, Café Fifty Three.

INTIMATE BUSINESS
The bar, inspired by the traditional "gentleman's club," but upbeat and not stuffy, features a new fireplace with marble facing sur-rounded by couches and cocktail seating. In addition, there is seating at the bar and a living-room-like sofa grouping.
Photographs by John Sutton.

DEFINED DINING
The renovated hotel has just one restaurant, Café Fifty Three, with a mural which continues the playing-card theme established by the Donald Salton prints in the bar (facing page, top). The restaurant is differentiated from the bar architecturally and opens onto the new rotunda (facing page, bottom). Seating areas within the restaurant are separated by bulkheads with planters to offer diners more privacy (above).
Photographs by John Sutton.

On upper floors, minor changes were made. Partitions were added in the meeting rooms, and one meeting room was converted into a richly detailed board room. A new circular stair was added from the second to the third floor to improve circulation between meeting rooms. Several guest rooms on the fourth floor were reconfigured to create the fitness center. Guest room floors have all new furniture and finishes, but no changes in partitions; in bathrooms, only the flooring, wall covering, lighting and mirrors were replaced.

Before the renovation, the interior had a range of styles in various spaces, including rattan and French provincial. The designers decided to apply a single look to the building, varying it but never crossing into other periods or styles. Because the exterior of the building is obviously so recent, authentic Art Deco or Moderne design would look out of place, so the design loosely recalls both aesthetics without being literal. Cognac-toned anegre wood paneling and moldings appear in many public spaces, and the whole hotel has custom-designed carpeting, often with patterns based on designs from books of the work of Art Deco designer Jacques Ruhlman. Light fixtures, many of which were custom-designed, echo the Deco-Moderne tone, although some are quite contemporary.

Materials, fabrics and colors were chosen to make spaces warm and sometimes clubby, but never stuffy, according to interior designer Cynthia Forchielli of Barry Design. Though jewel-tone colors often appear in carpets and fabrics, and guest room walls are rich blues, garnets, and celadon, the effect is always tailored and masculine. "It's friendly and welcoming but not fussy," said Forchielli. "This is a businessman's hotel."

CLUB CORRIDOR
A small corridor connecting the group and main registration areas with the news shop suggests a private club with its exaggerated black house telephone desk and lamps.
Photograph by John Sutton.

CONTEMPORARY CLASSICS
Guest bedrooms feature anegre furniture and fixtures which loosely recall Streamline Moderne design. Although tapestry fabrics on lounge chairs depart from the geometric patterns found in many of the custom fabrics and carpets in the hotel, they strike a tailored tone and complement the businesslike room.
Photograph by John Sutton.

Sheraton Palace

San Francisco, California

When owner Kyo-ya Company Ltd.,
originally decided to renovate the
Sheraton Palace Hotel in San Francisco, it
had architect Skidmore, Owings &
Merrill do studies for an addition rising
dramatically above the back of the existing
1909 building. When the renovated hotel
reopened in 1991, the tower was nowhere
to be seen, but $150 million of preserva-
tion work allowed management to reposition the historic property into more
lucrative business traveler and high-end
social markets.

Name	Sheraton Palace Hotel
Location	San Francisco, California
Owner	Kyo-Ya Company, Ltd.
Operator	ITT Sheraton Corporation
Type of Hotel	Luxury / Business
Date of Original Construction	1909
Number of Rooms	552
Bars & Restaurants	3 restaurants, each with bar
Meeting Rooms	
Number & Size	22 rooms / 45,000 square feet
Recreation Facilities	Indoor pool, exercise machines, spa
Type of Renovation	Complete; operations shut down
Cost	$150 million
Date	January 1989 - April 1991
Architect	Architect: Skidmore, Owings & Merrill, San Francisco, California Historical Architect: Page & Turnbull, San Francisco, California
Consultants	Food Service: Abrams & Tanaka Associates
Contractor	Takenaka USA

IMPROVED RECEPTION
*The registration desk, originally tucked off in a corner where the main
entrance of the hotel meets the main corridor, has a new, open
lobby with a much larger desk and a separate seating area. The new
barrel-vaulted ceiling gives guests a preview of the Sunset Court
and the swimming pool.*
Photograph by Jon Miller, © Hedrich-Blessing.

OUTWARDLY UNCHANGED
Although considerable work went into repairing deterioration of the limestone wall facing and cornice at the first floor and earthquake damage to the brick walls and terra cotta window sills above, the overall appearance of the hotel's primary facades changed little in the renovation.
Photograph by Jon Miller, © Hedrich-Blessing.

INTRODUCING A NEW PAST
Although most of the building exterior was painstakingly restored to its original appearance, designers exercised their creativity on the new entry canopy. Inspired by the original marquise, which had been removed years before the renovation, it has clean lines and dramatic lighting to make it stand out from the existing building.
Photograph by Jon Miller, © Hedrich-Blessing.

Overlooked by the media in all the attention to hotel history restored, but not by the guests of the renovated hotel, were major new features housed in an addition which replaced a decades-old expansion at the back of the hotel, removed early in the renovation process. These included an indoor swimming pool and health spa, 10,000 square feet of meeting rooms, and a business center - all key parts in the strategy to attract more meetings and business travelers. "We have the best of both worlds now," said Jim Kilroy, director of marketing for the Sheraton Palace. "The charm and ambiance of a landmark historic hotel, with all the amenities travelers are looking for today."

Offering all the amenities had been a trademark for the hotel for a generation before the existing building was constructed. Two prominent Westerners, William Ralston and William Sharon, put San Francisco on the map for demanding travelers when they built the first Palace Hotel in 1875, complete with a seven-story skylighted interior carriage entrance court and five hydraulic elevators. The building was a hit with travelers, but it burned in the fire following the 1906 earthquake and was demolished. The present building, designed by Trowbridge and Livingston (designers of the St. Regis Hotel in New York), opened in 1909.

But by 1989, it was a "tired, eighty-year-old building. Dowdy." as Kilroy put it. Teaming up with San Francisco preservation architects Page & Turnbull, Skidmore decided to restore the exterior of the building and the most important public rooms, including the landmark Garden Court, a 5,000 square foot enclosed courtyard with an art glass ceiling. The cost for restoring the ceiling was $7 million, which involved removing it panel by panel, restoring it in an artisan's studio, and then reinstalling it. The off-site work proved doubly worthwhile because it meant the ceiling panels were not in the building when the Loma Prieta earthquake struck in October 1989, causing significant damage to the building.

CENTRAL SPLENDOR
The centerpiece of the hotel is the Garden Court, with its 8,000 square foot art glass ceiling and classical marble columns. San Francisco's only listed indoor landmark space, it predates the present hotel, having been a skylighted carriage entrance surrounded by balconies (above) in the previous hotel constructed on the same site in 1875, which was destroyed in the fire caused by the 1906 earthquake. Although the Garden Court (left) looked very similar after the renovation to its appearance when the hotel opened in 1909, massive effort and expense were lavished on its restoration. The ceiling glass was removed for cleaning and restoration in a stained glass specialist's studio - and thus spared from all damage in the 1989 San Francisco earthquake. The special faux-limestone plaster walls were renewed, and decorative niches were stripped of non-historic gold leaf and strengthened to resist earthquakes.
Renovation photograph by Jon Miller, © Hedrich-Blessing.

PATH OF TIME
The main corridor leads from the entrance on San Francisco's prime thoroughfare, Market Street, past the hotel's main entry lobby and the Garden Court, and on to ballrooms and the entry to second floor meeting rooms. The faux limestone walls with marble wainscot look like the ones seen in a historic photograph of the corridor (right), but many of them were actually rebuilt during the renovation (below) because of damage caused by the 1989 earthquake.
Renovation photograph by Jon Miller, © Hedrich-Blessing.

HOW TO DRAW A CROWD
*Maxfield Parrish's The Pied Piper,
which had hung in the hotel ever
since its construction, is the
centerpiece of the bar in the new
Maxfield's restaurant (below). The
original skylight and mosaic floor
were uncovered during the renovation, and the coffered ceiling was
refinished. The adjoining dining area
visible through the doorway at the
end of the room (opposite page)
features an exhibition kitchen in a
glass and dark wood enclosure. The
original Pied Piper Bar (left),
photographed around 1915 has the
same dark wood and leather theme,
but takes it a few steps further.*
Renovation photographs by
Jon Miller, © Hedrich-Blessing

Page & Turnbull meticulously analyzed and replicated original materials in the Garden Court and the adjoining French Parlors and on the exterior of the building. A lengthy search led the architects to Nevada for stone to match the original where damage had occurred on the exterior over the years, while research produced a multi-pronged solution to the dilemma of how to strengthen the historic terra cotta window sills so they would not break in earthquakes.

While the renovation team was busy preserving the exterior and historic spaces in the building, it was reworking the design of guest rooms and less historic spaces and creating an all new look for the addition. The swimming pool and a new breakout room for the meeting rooms on the second floor are unmistakably modern, but they echo the Garden Court with their huge barrel-vaulted skylights. The formal ground floor corridors of the building were preserved with subtle changes to accommodate technical requirements and a palette of colors and materials which fit contemporary taste.

Skidmore designers used new materials and existing treasures such as a mosaic tile floor to create the Pied Piper Bar and Maxfield's Restaurant around the original Maxfield Parrish painting, which had been a much-loved fixture in the building for decades. Architect Hideto Horiike used an Asian-flavored design in the new Kyo-ya Restaurant, a Japanese eatery that replaced one of the ground-floor restaurants, which was not retained in the renovation.

ROOM FOR REINTERPRETATION

Guest-room walls stayed in place during the renovation - but just about everything else changed. Four-poster beds, oversized armchairs with ottomans and rich wood grain case goods set a tone of luxury, while muted wall colors and fabrics complement the restrained style used throughout the building. A guest room photographed in 1915 (above) has many of the same elements, but the lighter weight furniture and dark stained trim give a more austere bent to the room.

Renovation photograph by Jon Miller, © Hedrich-Blessing

SPECIAL ELAN
Bathrooms were gutted, but like guest rooms, their walls
remained intact through the renovation, precluding a four or five
fixture layout. To provide the substance of luxury within that
constraint, designers crafted marble and polychrome
metal vanities.
Photograph by Jon Miller, © Hedrich-Blessing

Guest-room floor layouts did not change, but all finishes and fixtures were removed and replaced. The mechanical, electrical and plumbing systems were gutted and replaced, as were kitchens and other back-of-the-house facilities. In addition to seismic improvements, the structure of the building received a major makeover in places where new support was needed for the addition with its swimming pool.

When the hotel reopened after 27 months, the original price tag and schedule for the renovation were long forgotten, largely because of damage caused by the earthquake. The history of the building was remembered by the public and the renovation was noticed by all. Operator ITT Sheraton Corp. raised its lowest room rates to $180 at the reopening and reduced its group tour bookings in favor of more business travelers and corporate meetings. The historical cachet drew back high-end San Francisco social functions which had abandoned the Sheraton Palace before the renovation; once again the property was on a par with its oldest and most famous competitors in the city. "We are the oldest hotel in the city," Kilroy said. "We feel the history of the Palace is unique. We truly are a landmark."

THE ROYAL UPDATE

Suites feature rich classical furniture and stately, muted colors to impart a sense of understated grandeur suitable for visiting royalty, but the interior design is not the original look, even if it looks timeless. A historic photograph (left) of an original suite shows more complex detailing, more furniture, and an overall appearance that looks busy to today's eye.

Renovation photograph by Jon Miller, © Hedrich-Blessing

HIGH DIVE

Perched atop the back of the hotel in place of additions from the 1930s which were demolished at the outset of the renovation, the new indoor swimming pool features a dramatic barrel-vaulted skylight. In addition to a whirlpool spa, the recreation center also includes an adjacent exercise room, sauna and locker rooms.

Photograph by Jon Miller, © Hedrich-Blessing.

SCRATCH THE SKIN

The walls and ceiling of the renovated Rose Room on the ground floor look familiar to longtime guests, but beneath their surface are massive new steel beams and columns supporting new meeting rooms and recreation facilities above - including a swimming pool. The walls and ceilings are actually brand new, because the original ballroom was leveled (after being carefully measured and cut apart for samples) to accommodate the new structural framing.

Photograph by Jon Miller, © Hedrich-Blessing.

MEETING EXPECTATIONS

A fixture in San Francisco's social life for more than a century, the Sheraton Palace had an established reputation for balls, dances and parties. The Gold Room retains its social connections, and to fulfill the requirements of the daytime market for meeting rooms, the renovation provided totally new audio-visual systems and improved food service facilities.

Photograph by Jon Miller, © Hedrich-Blessing.

SIGNATURE SPACE
The Sunset Court subtly reflects the design of the historic Garden Court; its skylight strongly resembles the one over the new swimming pool, which is nearby. This new second floor breakout area is surrounded by new meeting rooms, and is connected to the ground floor by a new escalator. Fritted glass in the skylight and abstracted classical columns refer to the design of the Garden Court without imitating it.
Photograph by Jon Miller, © Hedrich-Blessing.

The Regent Beverly Wilshire
Beverly Hills, California

If it isn't easy being pretty, it's back-breaking work being beautiful. Nobody knows that better than the owners and designers who in 1987 set out to renovate the Regent Beverly Wilshire, a landmark of Los Angeles glamour which was in danger of being out-glittered by some of its neighboring rivals. The Regent chain, based in Asia, needed to make sure the property would hold its own against any in the sybaritic Los Angeles market. Sitting on Wilshire Boulevard at the foot of Rodeo Drive, the Beverly Wilshire had an unbeatable location and a regal history, thanks to the traditional design by architects Walker and Eisen, sumptuous building materials such as Carrara marble from Italy, and a clientele dominated by rulers of Hollywood, with a sprinkling of genuine royalty from abroad.

FACIAL, NOT FACELIFT
Long a presence on Wilshire Boulevard at the foot of Rodeo Drive, the hotel's original building, now known as the Wilshire Wing, was rejuvenated but not altered greatly on the exterior during the renovation. The designers reinforced the Rodeo Drive location by retaining the primary pedestrian entrance on the original facade shown here.
Photograph by Jaime Ardilles-Arce.

Name	**The Regent Beverly Wilshire**
Location	**Beverly Hills, California**
Owner	**Hotel Investment Corporation**
Operator	**Regent Hotels International**
Type of Hotel	**Luxury**
Date of Original Construction	**1928**
Number of Rooms	**300**
Bars & Restaurants	**4**
Meeting Rooms Number & Size	**9 / 25,500 square feet**
Recreation Facilities	**Pool, free weights, exercise machines, health and beauty treatments**
Type of Renovation	**Phased, hotel open during construction**
Cost	**$100 million**
Date	**1987 - 1993**
Architect	**Gruen Associates, Los Angeles, California**
Interior Designer	**Project Associates, Beverly Hills, California**
Consultants	**Decoration: Betty Garber, Westwood, California**
Contractor	**Peck/Jones, Los Angeles, California**

PAMPERED APPEARANCE
The renovation did not leave shops as raw space for tenants to finish on their own. The florist space near the Café features a trompe l'oeil ceiling mural (top).
Photograph by Jaime Ardilles-Arce.

REDEFINING THE CENTER
The renovated lobby is much larger than the original lobby and reinforces the sense of hierarchy in the ground floor design. The two story space is surrounded by hotel services and concessions and sets the tone for the interior of the building with three-color marble flooring, intricate woodwork and antique furniture.
Photograph by Jaime Ardilles-Arce.

The hotel prospered, but years of additions and remodelings made it a muddle of expensive materials rather than a palace of fine design. Regent decided to bring the blur of styles and schemes into stunning, opulent focus, and turned the challenge over to architect Kurt Franzen of Gruen Associates and interior designer Glenn Texeira of Project Associates. Major programmatic elements included a new pool and elaborate spa and a guest-room upgrade which reduced the count in the original part of the property from 248 to 148.

The designers had an ample budget and could start with a clean slate inside the building, but they had to work within the constraints of the structural layout, exterior architecture and site design of the original Italian Renaissance build-ing, and a bland 1971 addition. That meant interior column spacings which did not align with window locations, facades which harmonized like a 1920s flapper wearing bell-bottom pants, and a fractured entry sequence which deposited guests who arrived by car at the back door of the main lobby on Rodeo Drive.

In place of the disarray in the interior design, the designers adopted a classic but not stuffy approach with the lavishness and easy-going classical elegance which is a trademark of Beverly Hills. Within this unified and even grandiose framework, the character, colors and styles of the individual spaces vary so that the hotel is dignified without being pompous or stiff. The color palette is rich but restrained, the furniture includes ornate antiques and more inviting reproductions, and acres of marble topped off with miles of moldings assure guests they are getting their money's worth at rates which start above $300.

LUXURY AND LEISURE
Located near the hotel lobby, the informal Lobby lounge offers afternoon tea, cocktails and light dining. Its interior features comfort-able leather chairs, sofas covered in melon velvet and Louis XVI round tables with inset antique rouge marble. The window treatment masks the structural misalignment between the interior columns and window openings on the exterior walls (above).
Photographs by Jaime Ardilles-Arce.

ELEGANCE EVERYWHERE
Luxury doesn't end with the lobby, as guests discover as soon as they enter the adjacent women's room and men's room. Dark wood paneling graces the men's room (bottom), while large vanities in the women's room accommodate guests who want to make a grand entrance (right). Both spaces have extensive marble in contrasting colors.
Photographs by Jaime Ardilles-Arce.

REPAST PERFECT

The Dining Room was one of the boldest moves made by the renovation designers to encourage the rich and famous to frequent the Beverly Wilshire. There are numerous clear views — and lots of obstructions — from table to table in the restaurant, so that anyone famous who eats there might — or might not — be seen by anyone else in the restaurant. Management promoted the operation as a center for "power dining" and Richard Hack of the Hollywood Reporter called it "the hottest lunch spot in town."
Photographs by Jaime Ardilles-Arce.

To clear up the architectural confusion, the designers revamped the layout of the major public spaces, introducing a recognizable hierarchy to guide guests through the inevitable complexity caused by the placement of the buildings on the site. The expanded main lobby facing Rodeo Drive is connected to the motor entrance on the opposite side of the building with a clear and finely-detailed sequence of spaces to make the link between the two entrances easy to find. A range of lounges, cafes and restaurants encourages visitors to explore the rest of the ground floor.

On the second floor, a new spa aims for the opulence one might expect from a Hong Kong luxury chain at its debut in Los Angeles. An outdoor pool, separate saunas and steam rooms for men and women, a sun deck and snack bar, a gym with free weights and exercise machines, and an array of beauty treatments and massages are intended to make guests want to spend a long time in the spa. Guests who don't want to leave at all can avail themselves of the two-bedroom cabana suite overlooking the sun deck.

TOP SHELF DETAILING
More than 150 woods went into the wall paneling and custom-fabricated French Bar with stools and separate stand-up bar. The Bar features Biedermeier and Regency furnishings, with chair upholstered in cognac leather and sofas in brown embossed velvet.
Photograph by Jaime Ardilles-Arce.

For those who would rather stay in a regular guest room, the renovated hotel provides large rooms with at least two televisions each, two-line telephones and electronic signals to summon a floor steward or keep staff from disturbing the occupants. The signature of the Regent chain is deluxe bathrooms; each marble bathroom in the Beverly Wilshire has a large soaking tub, a separate shower, a telephone, a scale, and a hair dryer. The 50 suites in the original part of the building have special furniture collections as well as additional sitting rooms or bedrooms. Rooms in the newer wing were renovated in a similar fashion; renovations proceeded on one floor at a time to allow the hotel to continue operating during construction.

Although the renovation set out to reduce the jumble and clutter of the building, it did not attempt to make the property a taut, relentless design statement. The goal was to match the worldwide standard for hotels, combining a European-inspired aesthetic, Asian levels of luxury, California informality and a Los Angeles-class of high-profile presentation. By varying the designs of the individual spaces but tying them loosely together with compatible styles and materials, the renovation offers luxury everywhere but in a relaxed way that implies that opulence is an assumption, not an assertion. This approach might be what guests would expect from an Asian-owned luxury hotel in Beverly Hills.

MEDITERRANEAN INSPIRATION
In renovating the 1971 Beverly wing, designers incorporated a new second floor pool, sun deck, and health spa. The interior of the spa strikes a contemporary note, while the pool takes its Mediterranean inspiration from Sophia Loren's pool in Italy (opposite page).
Photograph by Jaime Ardilles-Arce.

DOWN-HOME L.A. CAFE
The most informal food and beverage operation in the hotel is the Cafe, where the Main Street USA drugstore meets Southern California conspicuous consumption. The result is striped floors in marble, Manuel Canovas fabric Roman shades, and espresso drinks as well as banana splits on the menu.
Photograph by Jaime Ardilles-Arce.

WHO NEEDS A PRESIDENT?

Some hotels seem overly optimistic naming suites "presidential" but at the Beverly Wilshire, the top suite has attracted a list which makes Presidents look like anti-climaxes. Woolworth heiress Barbara Hutton lived there, and other guests included Elvis Presley, Elton John, Ringo Starr, Andrew Lloyd Webber, Stevie Nicks and enough foreign royalty to qualify the suite as an international palace. With a square footage - and daily rate - of 4,000, it has a living room, a dining room, two sitting rooms, two bedrooms, and two and a half baths. Interior themes range from formal European furniture with Oriental influences in the living room (top left, facing page), to the English estate tone of the dining room (top, this page). The library adds a touch of elegance, with its airy feeling that avoids the academic look of dark wood shelves (left, this page). The spaces in the suite are united by the grand central hall, reminiscent of a 19th-century mansion with its inlaid wood floor and Corinthian columns (bottom, facing page).

Photographs by Jaime Ardilles-Arce.

WHO NEEDS A PRESIDENT?
*The bedrooms are more American and comfortable,
with a big sofa and lots of pillows in the master
bedroom (above) and comfortable chairs in the second
bedroom (bottom). The Regent chain's obsession with
bathrooms shows up in its full glory in the master
bathroom, where oversized vanity mirrors give the
illusion of even more marble than the room actually has
(right). A marble vanity with three-way mirror caters to
guests who want to set fashion firsts, whether or not
they happen to be First Lady (p. 84, top right).*
Photographs by Jaime Ardilles-Arce.

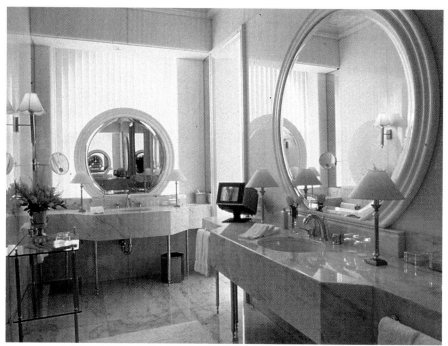

EASY-GOING OPULENCE

The Regent Beverly Wilshire offers three categories of suites and three categories of bedrooms. Suites (top right) tend toward the more formal, while guest rooms (center) show their comfortable side first; both emphasize high-grade materials and low-key detailing which avoids the overbearing look of a period reproduction interior. Suites and guest rooms are designed in four color themes: wheat, peach, rose and celery. A large one-room suite is known as the Warren Beatty suite for the famous actor who lived there for long periods (below).

Photographs by Jaime Ardilles-Arce.

The Beverly Prescott Hotel
Los Angeles, California

How do you fit a traditional-style urban boutique hotel into the city with a soul of trend-setting youthfulness and a body of suburban sprawl?

Buying old hotels in the center of the city and renovating each property with an individual flavor launched Bill Kimpton as a hotel entrepreneur in San Francisco and later in Portland and Seattle. But Kimpton interpreted his own formula slightly differently when he continued to Los Angeles, where old just means anything that's not brand new, and there is no city center. So instead of renovating an architecturally rich historic property in downtown Los Angeles like the Checkers Hotel, Kimpton bought a humdrum thirty-year-old hotel on the west side of the city.

Name	The Beverly Prescott Hotel
Location	Los Angeles, California
Owner	B.I.L.
Operator	Kimpton Hotel and Restaurant Group, Inc.
Type of Hotel	Boutique
Date of Original Construction	1961
Number of Rooms	140
Bars & Restaurants	Rox Restaurant
Meeting Rooms (Number & Size)	2 / 5,300 square feet
Recreation Facilities	Outdoor pool, exercise cycles, rowing machines, step aerobics
Type of Renovation	Hotel shut down during construction
Cost	$12.5 million
Date Completed	April 1993
Architect	Three Architecture
Interior Designer	Hotel: Cheryl Rowley Interior Design, Beverly Hills with Patrick de Monfreid Restaurant, pool & rooftop meeting room: Ron Leiberman, Design Development Co., Tarzana, California
Consultants	Mechanical Engineer: Tom Gilbertson and Associates, Moraga, California
Contractor	R.D. Olson Construction, Anaheim, California

SOUTHERN CALIFORNIA
If a Southern California hotel isn't on the beach, it's sure to have a pool. The renovation added stone paving to the patio around the existing pool, and fitted it out with canvas cabanas and decorative lanterns (below). The entire exterior was painted one color (facing page) to reduce the high-rise boxiness it had before the renovation (left).
Renovation photographs by Fred Licht Photography;
pre-renovation photographs by Kimpton Hotel and Restaurant Group, Inc.

Kimpton decided to market his new Beverly Prescott hotel to the younger segment of the entertainment industry concentrated nearby in Beverly Hills, Century City and West Hollywood, appealing to those on the way up, but not too far up the ladder to appreciate an informal, relaxing property with moderate prices. The next step was to make the former Beverly Hillcrest Hotel into a Kimpton hotel. Built in 1961, the twelve-story structure had a blah "contemporary" exterior of that period and an interior that ran the gamut of mediocre design from the past three decades: rust color shag carpets with red flocked wallpaper, French provincial furniture, and a recently redone beige-on-beige lobby.

Kimpton commissioned designer Cheryl Rowley to make the property into "an emotional adventure unlike any hotel in Los Angeles." She set out to give Los Angeles something new because she was "tired of seeing very beige hotel properties." The ground floor was gutted, but the exterior and partitions on the guest room floors were left almost unchanged, so Rowley had the challenge of redefining the property mostly through interior design.

She chose a bright and lively palette and an eclectic blend of finishes and furnishings to enliven the spaces and give them a strong Southern California character. A new entry loggia provided a transition between the existing porte cochere and the lobby. The "living room" with fireplace—a standard feature in Kimpton hotels—was separated from the circulation path, and touches like limestone flooring that begins in the exterior loggia and continues into the lobby create an indoor-outdoor connection that complements the bright colors to lighten the lobby and make it authentically Southern Californian.

YOU'VE ARRIVED
Before the renovation, the doors at the porte cochere led directly into the lobby. To give guests a more defined sense of arrival and entry, designer Cheryl Rowe created a covered exterior Loggia with outdoor furniture (top). Upon entering the lobby, guests find a stopping space focused on a gossamer day bed (right).
Photographs by Fred Licht Photography.

HOME SWEET HOME
Every Kimpton hotel lobby has a comfortable "living room" with a fireplace; the Beverly Prescott provides this traditional touch while maintaining its eclectic Los Angeles nuance through eclectic, whimsical lamps and objets d'art and furniture and fabrics which blend traditional and current styles.
Photographs by Fred Licht Photography

Guest rooms were divided into two themes, one geared to men and one to women. To compensate for the limited size of the bathrooms, which were not changed, Rowley added a small wall to create an entry foyer adjacent to them in each room. Guest room doors have a leather strap and a leather and chrome tag for the room number, inspired by the hardware found on luggage.

Like all Kimpton hotels, the Beverly Prescott has a restaurant with its own name, operation and personality. Ron Leiberman, hired to do the restaurants in several previous Kimpton hotel projects, was brought in to design the restaurant, rooftop meeting room, and pool. Leiberman gave the Rox Restaurant a subdued spirit, with natural materials and colors drawn from the native landscape of Southern California. Guests enter through a patio area with a bougainvillea arbor and wrought iron gates to reach the dining area with coffered ceilings and cherrywood floors.

CONTRASTING SUITES
The property's twelve suites include two geared toward business travelers, with a large round table for meetings and restrained furniture and colors (above). The deluxe suite, marketed to individual travelers, strikes a more romantic tone, with floral fabrics and chaise lounges (right).
Photographs by Fred Licht Photography

HIS AND HERS

To appeal to male and female business travelers, the hotel has two guest room schemes, the "stripe" room with a feminine touches like floral drapes (below) and the "checkerboard" room, named for its bold, graphic headboard design (facing page). Case goods are mahogany with gold accents, with some fruitwood pieces. Nightstands are hand-painted to resemble draped fabric. Although each room has full-wall sliding glass doors onto its balcony, the extensive drapery gives the renovated rooms a more intimate feeling than the original modern building had (left).

Renovation photographs by Fred Licht Photography; pre-renovation photographs by Kimpton Hotel and Restaurant Group, Inc.

GARDEN VARIETY
Guest rooms feature a granite-topped cast stone pullman in the bathroom instead of a conventional vanity. The piece is inspired by garden consoles.

Bancroft Hotel
Berkeley, California

Many renovations strive to change a hotel building to fend off an unwanted change in the business which occupies it, but at the Bancroft Hotel, the renovation made the building appear unchanged so that it could house an entirely new operation. The Bancroft, which was not designed as a hotel but became one after a $2 million restoration, still looks remarkably similar to the way it looked when it was completed in 1928. Continuity was the watchword of the renovation, both out of necessity and by design, allowing the owner to keep a tight budget and offer a product tailored to its local market niche.

Name	**Bancroft Hotel**
Location	**Berkeley, California**
Owner	**Ross Family**
Operator	**Martin Ross**
Type of Hotel	**Small / Moderate Price**
Date of Original Construction	**1928**
Number of Rooms	**22**
Bars & Restaurants	**None**
Meeting Rooms **Number & Size**	**1 / 4,000 square feet**
Recreation Facilities	**None**
Type of Renovation	**Conversion from sorority house**
Cost	**$2 million**
Date	**October 1992 - November 1993**
Architect	**Berger Detmer Architects, San Francisco, California**
Interior Designer	**Candra Scott & Associates, San Francisco, California**
Consultants	**Historic Preservation: Randolph Langenbach, Berkeley, California** **Structural Engineer: Steven Tipping & Associates, Emeryville, California**
Contractor	**Ryan Associates, San Francisco, California**

NOCTURNAL ACTIVITY
By day, few major changes made during the renovation are visible on the exterior of the building. At night, extensive new lighting draws the eye to the features of the street facade (below) and welcomes guests to the main entrance (opposite page).
Photographs by Andrew McKinney.

The former College Women's Club building is a fixture of its neighborhood, dating from the same period as the historic buildings on the University of California campus across the street. Designed by Walter T. Steilberg, a noted California architect, the building had the classic but subtly eclectic design of the golden age of San Francisco Bay Area architecture. Constructed as a university women's club, it had meeting space, a dining room, lounges and sleeping rooms. Developer Martin Ross, whose family had owned the building since the late 1970s, decided to convert the structure into a hotel after a series of other uses which followed the demise of the women's club in 1973. Hospitality offered a higher profit than the likely alternatives, and preservation of the historic aspects of the building offered not only marketable cachet in the history-conscious Bay Area, but ready development approval from city officials and a twenty percent federal tax credit for the cost of the project.

The existing building translated easily into hotel use, except the diminutive sleeping rooms - sized for single visiting scholars in the 1920s, not hotel guests in the 1990s. Reducing the number of guest rooms to allow an increase in room size did not make sense because there were only twenty-two rooms to begin with, and getting approvals for an addition to the building would be very difficult.

IMAGES OF THE EAST
Architect Walter Steilberg incorporated many Chinese influences in the original design of the building, an approach which was continued in the renovation design. The Chinese-inspired guest room furniture was custom-built based on designs originally drawn by Steilberg. The Chinese theme is not overpowering; draperies and bedspreads are damask, and the small chandeliers (not visible) from the 1920s came from a local salvage yard.
Photograph by Andrew McKinney.

UNCERTAINTY OF AGE

The old appearance of the lobby is authentic overall, but many of the individual elements changed in the renovation. The ceiling was disassembled then reinstalled one foot lower following installation of new structural elements and insulation. The furniture is antique, but acquired during the renovation. The chandeliers, original to the building, were rewired and fitted with mica during the renovation. The iron standing lamps have custom shades with Latin calligraphy, giving the room a warm light and an erudite feeling (bottom). Fabrics for the sofas and armchairs are cut-velvets, tapestries and mohair. The lobby is one end of the main meeting room, which is usually vacant when not in use (right).

Renovation photographs by Andrew McKinney.

And sixty-five years after its construction, the building needed a costly update of finishes and systems, so the renovation team did not have the luxury of reconfiguring the interior anyway. The key to making the existing rooms appealing, said architect Miles Berger, was to capitalize on charm, making guests focus on the authenticity of the historic design rather than the size of the rooms.

The visible result of the renovation is a careful retention of original features, with new elements detailed to imitate or complement the existing ones. When building on the eclectic motifs and influences in the building, interior designer Candra Scott avoided the often-revived Arts and Crafts movement and emphasized other ones to distinguish the project from the instant-old-looking buildings popping up like mushrooms in the Bay Area. Guest-room furniture was custom built on previously-unexecuted designs by Steilberg identified by the project team during its research. Steilberg, who collected Chinese antiques and researched and photographed Chinese decorative arts for decades, used Chinese materials and motifs prominently in the building. The renovation continued this theme, commissioning Chinese-style art for the guest rooms and using a Chinese design from the 1930s as the basis for the pattern of the custom Axminster carpeting.

CALIFORNIA CLASSIC
The Bancroft is a good example of the homegrown style of architecture which evolved in California in the early 20th century, mixing elements of the Mediterranean, Classical, and Arts and Crafts styles. Details like the projecting top story and the lattice spandrel panels below the windows make the basically rectangular building look like much more than a box and the variety of balconies make the small rooms seem special (above). The biggest change on the exterior since the early days has been the maturation of the trees and shrubs (facing page).
Renovation photographs by Andrew McKinney.

The basement, which originally housed a cafeteria, was renovated as leased office space. There are new rest rooms and a new coat room in the basement, and the owner hopes to add a restaurant there or possibly on the first floor. New ramps and a wheelchair lift made the basement accessible to the handicapped; additional measures brought the ground floor up to accessibility standards, but the upper two floors of sleeping rooms were not included in the accessibility program because of the lack of space for an elevator and accessible bathrooms. In addition to a new roof and a new coat of paint, exterior work included rebuilding some of the decks and balconies and renewing landscape elements.

The renovation also included much work that is not visible, from a new roof to new foundations, new electrical and plumbing supply systems, plaster and stucco. Most difficult was the seismic upgrade, which necessitated dismantling the coffered ceiling in the main meeting room to allow installation of a new structural diaphragm and steel moment frame. While the ceiling was open, new sound insulation went in, along with new lighting and a new audio system. This subtle camouflage of major changes in the building typifies the approach taken in the renovation, which offers guests the now-trendy club-like atmosphere more by keeping the old look than by adding a new look.

Hall, College Women's Club
Berkeley, Calif.

COZY WELCOME
The entry lobby typifies the spare but plastic interpretation of Mediterranean architecture made famous by Julia Morgan, architect of William Randolph Hearst's San Simeon castle. Walter Steilberg, architect of the Bancroft, worked in Morgan's office before starting his own practice. The biggest change made during the renovation was the addition of a custom-pattern carpet.
Renovation photographs by Andrew McKinney.

Hilton Hawaiian Village
Honolulu, Hawaii

For Hilton Hawaiian Village on Honolulu's Waikiki Beach, with 2,500 guest rooms, 80,000 square feet of meeting space and more than 75 retail spaces in about two dozen buildings on 22 acres, renovation is as routine as laundry. And at this scale, a major renovation poses almost superhuman challenges: how to reposition the long-time largest property in the state, how to coordinate construction in a maze of buildings ranging from thatched hut to 35-story high-rise, and how to give a new look to a site where a motley crew of structures has been accumulating for 60 years. Enthusiastic after completing the latest tower on the property and vigilant as they saw luxury mega-resorts proliferate in Hawaii, co-owners Hilton Hotel Corporation and Prudential Insurance Company of America decided in 1982 to take on the challenge of renovating Hilton Hawaiian Village, as part of an overall $1-billion upgrade program for existing Hilton properties in the United States.

WATER, WATER EVERYWHERE
The renovation left the oceanfront Rainbow Tower practically surrounded by water. The new double "super pool" is in the foreground, while the Hilton Lagoon is behind the tower to the right, with the Pacific Ocean and Waikiki Beach beyond.
Photography by Karen Suenaga for WAT&G.

Name	**Hilton Hawaiian Village**
Location	**Honolulu, Hawaii**
Owner	**Hilton Hotels Corporation**
	Prudential Insurance Company of America
Operator	**Hilton Hotels Corporation**
Type of Hotel	**Resort**
Date of Original Construction	**Pierpont Hotel built in 1920s. Hotel and neighboring cottages incorporated into village in 1954; Hilton operation in 1961.**
Number of Rooms	**2,542**
Bars & Restaurants (hotel operated)	**6 restaurants / 10 bars**
Meeting Rooms (Number & Size)	**11 divisible into 33 / 60,464 usable square feet; 82,359 square feet including breakout and outdoor areas**
Recreation Facilities	**Pools, exercise area, gym, spa, ocean beach, private dock with catamaran, submarines and other boats**
Type of Renovation	**Phased, hotel open throughout**
Cost	**$102 million**
Date Construction	**1986-1988**
Architect	**Wimberly Allison Tong & Goo, Honolulu, Hawaii**
Interior Designer	**Public Spaces: Hirsch Bedner & Associates Guest Rooms: Hilton Design Consultants Landscape Architect: Woolsey, Miyabara & Associates, Inc. Structural Engineer: Martin & Bravo, Inc. Mechanical Engineer: Ferris & Hamig Hawaii, Inc. Electrical Engineer: Douglas V. MacMahon, Ltd. Lighting Design: Grenald Associates**
Contractor	**Albert C. Kobayashi, Inc.**

The renovation project was appropriately named the Hilton Hawaiian Village Master Plan. It would take four years to design and two years to construct, at a cost of $102 million. Involving demolition, new construction, renovation of existing buildings, landscaping, and site and utility work, the plan was divided into four phases so that the property could remain in operation throughout construction. Definitely a make-over and not an expansion, the project brought a net loss of 37 guest rooms and about 50,000 square feet of building—but it increased open space on the site by 20 percent and transformed standard rooms to luxury. Although the changes run the gamut, there were a few goals which unified the project:

• Add order to the overall property
• Emphasize the beachfront Hawaiian setting in site layout and landscaping
• Improve and expand public spaces and recreation facilities, linking them with food and beverage outlets
• Upgrade the guest rooms, pushing the property's market range higher
• Improve the central lobby and arrival experience

Many of the components of the project fulfilled more than one of these goals, the site layout being the best example. The site is roughly a square, with the west side formed by the ocean and a lagoon dug in the 1950s at the order of industrialist Henry Kaiser, then owner of the hotel. Two guest room towers line the south side, while a seven story garage and conference center building dominates the north side. In between, a fourth guest room tower straddles the shore between the ocean and the lagoon, the center of the site is divided between low buildings and landscaped outdoor areas, and a fourth guest room tower with a low-rise meeting room wing takes up the east end of the site. Kaiser launched the "Hawaiian Village" concept by adding authentic-looking Hawaiian- and Polynesian-style buildings to an existing hotel, but in the following decades, an army of buildings gradually choked off the open space. The variety of sizes, shapes, colors and align-ments, compounded by the contrast between the towers and the lower build-ings, added up to what the master plan architects, Wimberly Allison Tong and Goo, diplomatically referred to as a mish-mash. Arriving guests couldn't even see that the property was on the ocean and got lost in the maze of buildings before reaching the beach.

The site design goal of maximizing openness and the connection with the beach was simple, but the constraints were powerful: the towers and parking garage were too large to demolish or move, while the low buildings between them provided essential retail and restaurant/lounge space—and the Hawaiian village theme itself. The design team had to make the most of the limited demolition which was feasible, so it decided to clear the center of the site, landscape it lavishly, and then make it the nexus of the programmatic elements of the master plan. The site now centers on an open-air one-story entry building constructed on a rise overlooking a 10,000 square foot "super pool" sur-rounded by stone terraces, gardens and naturalistic fountains, connecting to Waikiki Beach and the Pacific Ocean. Arriving guests can look through the building to the pool and the beach, with views of other landscaped areas on the site to either side. Three new bars and two new restaurants adjoin or overlook the new centerpiece on three sides.

The goal of unifying the property visually meant that the new entry building and other new construction could not be decked out in the thatched-roof garb used decades ago by Kaiser, because of the contrast that they would make with the high-rise buildings. The new construction is simple, somewhat ambiguously modern, with materials and detailing chosen to reinforce the Hawaiian theme, and lots of open-air spaces and heavy landscaping, indoors and out. The landscaping includes 300 kinds of plants, with area fauna ranging from penguins, flamingos, ducks and macaws to ornamental koi carp. The centerpiece of the landscape scheme is the new "super pool," actually two swimming pools surrounded by a stone sunbathing deck, lava grottoes and carp ponds.

The most striking use of the indoor-outdoor concept was in the Rainbow Tower, where the lagoon frontage of the building housed kitchen and laundry facilities before the renovation. The designers removed these back-of-the-house facilities to make room for meeting rooms

CHEESEBURGER IN PARADISE
The most popular restaurant in the renovated hotel is the Rainbow Lanai, an informal three-meal eatery surrounded by a koi pond. It features a buffet breakfast, as well as light fare such as hamburgers and cheeseburgers. The lanai (Hawaiian for porch or deck) adjoins the new "super" pool and the beach, and stretches below the balcony of the fine dining Bali-by-the-Sea restaurant (interior, rear).
Photograph by Augie Salbosa.

CLEARING AWAY CLUTTER
The existing ground level
plan of Hilton Hawaiian
Village before the renovation
shows a handful of major
structures along the edges of
the site — and a swarm of
smaller ones choking off
much of the space in
between. The ground level
Master Plan shows the
"super pool" and landscaping made possible by
demolition of low buildings
in an area strategically
located at the center of the
property.
Drawings by Wimberly Allison
Tong & Goo (WAT&G).

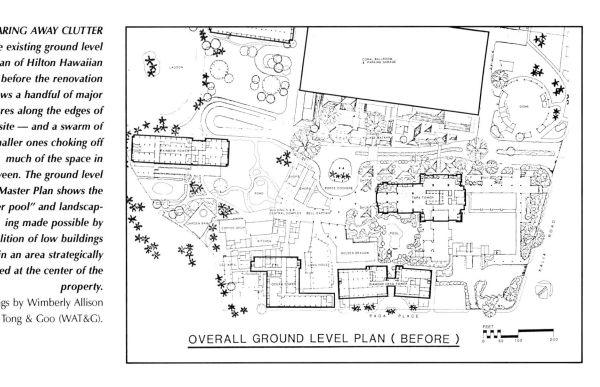

OVERALL GROUND LEVEL PLAN (BEFORE)

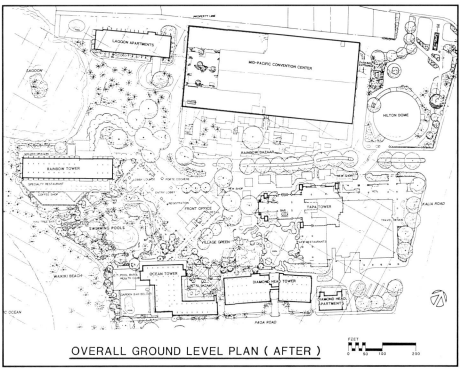

OVERALL GROUND LEVEL PLAN (AFTER)

and the hotel's Cantonese restaurant, the Golden Dragon. On the other side of the building, they extended the bottom two stories of the building to accommodate the fine dining restaurant, Bali-by-the-Sea, and the Rainbow Lanai, a new informal three-meal-a-day restaurant which quickly became the busiest at the property.

While the site design and landscaping concentrated on artfully recasting the property within its existing form, design-ers faced few restraints in renovating the

Ocean Tower — and stripped it to the bones. Before the renovation, the 300,000 square foot 1956 structure had 282 standard rooms. The makeover added two stories to the guest tower and replaced an adjacent apartment building with a two-story wing housing a bar, a cabaret, a discotheque and a health club with a roof-top pool. The renovation replaced a transmitter penthouse on the tower with two additional guest room floors, added two elevators, removed 14 meeting rooms, and increased the room count to 348.

Renamed Ali'i Tower (Hawaiian for "royalty") and placed in Hilton's top-of-the-market "Towers" product line the building offers guests a separate registra-tion lobby, rooms with marble baths, mini-bars and coffee makers, and exclusive use of the health club and rooftop pool. Two other guest room towers, the 782 guest room, 1967 Rainbow Tower and the 380 guest room, 1960 Diamond Head Tower, were also renovated, with new finishes in rooms and public areas as well as infrastructure upgrades.

SWITCHING BASES
Before the renovation, the bottom floors of the Rainbow Tower had a weak visual connection with the nearby lagoon (foreground, top). The ground floor was almost windowless and housed only back-of-the-house spaces, while the restaurant on the next level looked beyond the lagoon shoreline more than at it. The renovation started by cleaning up the lagoon and planting palm trees along the shore, then extended the building toward it with spaces which draw guests into contact with the water (center, after renovation). The Golden Dragon Restaurant has a large deck for outdoor dining with red pagoda-like shade structures (bottom), while the ground-level meeting rooms below it all open onto the lagoon and a private garden.

Before photo by WAT&G; after photos by Karen Suenaga for WAT&G.

TUNNEL VISION
Sitting on top of six levels of parking garage, the convention center is a long haul from the rest of the property. The escalators which connect it to ground level were formerly hidden in metal-clad enclosures reminiscent of 1970s stadiums (bottom). The renovation replaced those structures with a new enclosure that lets meeting-goers see the light at the end of the tunnel (left).
Before photo by WAT&G; after photo by Karen Suenaga for WAT&G.

The hotel's conference center, located above the parking garage, received a major workover of existing function rooms, the pre-function area, and the kitchen. Adjacent garage space was leveled and converted into a 6,000 square foot junior ballroom, the South Pacific, with new adjoining breakout space and meeting rooms. Site infrastructure work included a tie-in to central mechanical and electrical equipment in the Tapa Tower through a new utility loop.

To keep hotel operations running smoothly at 85 percent occupancy during construction, signs and barriers directed guests away from construction areas during each phase. An architectural model, signs, and newsletters kept guests informed about what was happening and why. Management gave guests chocolates and coupon books and threw weekly construction parties with entertainment. Complaints averaged twelve a day. Individual guests were not notified in advance of the renovation; groups were warned. One group insisted on management stopping construction during its one-week stay.

The physical renovation was accompanied by a revision of the rest of the property's product. To bolster its Hawaiian theme, the hotel recruited native Hawaiian artisans and crafts specialists to work in residence on site, and instituted a Hawaiian culture training program for its employees.

Management pronounced the completed renovation a success — and followed up with the predictable sequel: a major expansion. Wimberly Allison Tong and Goo received the commission to study where a new tower could be located to build the site out to the floor area ratio allowed by planning regulations for Waikiki. They recommended replacing the 1957 geodesic showroom dome with a 25-story, 400 room tower tailored for the business travel market. The hotel also

embarked on design and state approvals for building a man-made reef to turn the lagoon into a tropical snorkeling area. Hilton adopted "Return to Paradise" as its theme in marketing the Master Plan Renovation to guests, but for management and its designers, the renovation work week in paradise always seems to last seven days.

ROOFSCAPE TO LANDSCAPE

Before the renovation, the beachfront Ocean Tower was hemmed in by a clutter of low buildings which choked most of the center of the property and made guests walk a labyrinthe to find the beach. The Ocean Tower (above) had an assortment of air-conditioning gear and a television transmission station and antenna on its roof — all in plain view from the balconies of the other three towers on the property. The renovation started by demolishing the low buildings, added the "super" pool (center) and copious landscaping, and then gutted the tower and renamed it the Ali'i Tower, complete with private sundeck and pool. The renovation cleared mechanical equipment off roofs as part of an effort to improve the views from upper story hotel rooms throughout Waikiki Beach.

Before photo by WAT&G; after photo by
Karen Suenaga for WAT&G.

Hotel Vintage Plaza
Portland, Oregon

Bill Kimpton became the best known innovator in San Francisco hospitality by buying small hotels in the center of that city, renovating each one with luxury touches and a relaxed, individual flavor, and offering competitive prices. When he began his expansion to Portland, Oregon, with a century-old downtown hotel, he hardly had to worry about differentiating it from his other properties. The building had been gutted and rehabbed into speculative office space almost a generation earlier, leaving the top floor ringed with sloping greenhouse windows and a modern atrium rising from the ground floor lobby to the roof.

Name	*Hotel Vintage Plaza*
Location	*Portland, Oregon*
Owner	*Portland Hotel Associates*
Operator	*Kimpton Hotel & Restaurant Group, Inc.*
Type of Hotel	*Boutique*
Date of Original Construction	*1894*
Number of Rooms	*107*
Bars & Restaurants	*Pazzo Restaurant*
Meeting Rooms (Number & Size)	*7 divisible into 9 / 4,000 square feet*
Recreation Facilities	*Exercise room with exercise cycles, step machine, rowing machine*
Type of Renovation	*Conversion from unfinished speculative office rehab of original hotel building*
Cost	*$14 million*
Date Reopened	*May, 1991*
Interior Designer	*Hotel: Nan Rosenblatt Interior Design, San Francisco, California* *Restaurant: Ron Leiberman, Design Development Co., Tarzana, California*
Consultants	*Mechanical Engineer: Tom Gilbertson and Associates, Moraga, California*
Contractor	*Baugh Construction, Portland, Oregon*

OUTWARDLY UNCHANGED
The renovation gutted the interior of the building, but kept the exterior in its historic condition—with the temporary addition of a rather noticeable announcement of the hotel's arrival.
Photograph by John Vaughn.

CORPORATE PERK
Kimpton Group requires a wood-burning fireplace in
every hotel lobby. The fireplace subtly reinforces the
wine theme through the color of its marble facing
and the floral relief over the mantel.
Photograph by John Vaughn.

Kimpton chose a wine theme to celebrate Oregon's growing stature in viticulture. A wine cellar would be installed in the lobby and each guest room would be named after an Oregon winery. All that remained was to flesh out the interior of the building to fit the Kimpton vision. Unfortunately, the one specific requirement for the lobby in Kimpton's credo of generous, but unstuffy, classical design is a wood-burning fireplace — not an atrium.

"That was our first challenge," said interior designer Nan Rosenblatt, who had already renovated several San Francisco Kimpton hotels when she took on the Portland property. Although the project called for gutting interior partitions throughout, the exterior envelope and the atrium had to stay. Her mission was to accommodate the traditional, comfortable look of a Kimpton hotel within the shell, complete with atrium and greenhouse windows.

The skylit atrium opens onto every floor of the building, and the designers decided to take advantage of its light without spending a fortune trying to remake it into a more conventional space. They painted everything in the same color, including the wall sconces and railings, and then added a mass of plants to soften the space. The atrium posed a particular challenge at the lobby, which the Kimpton approach always details with a comfortable "living room." To create warmth and intimacy, Rosenblatt created two sitting areas, one oriented to the fireplace and one to a music area where a pianist plays a baby grand. Both turn their backs on the atrium, allowing guests to enjoy the light without looking at the towering, modern space itself.

The previous renovations of the building also complicated the meeting space design. There, windows spanning between two floors presented a challenge, exposing the legs and knees of those trying to do business to the view of passersby.

SIDE ATTRACTION
Kimpton hotels stress lots of amenities in an easy-going, tried-and-true atmosphere, not sleek styling and dazzling, soaring spaces. Instead of focusing the new lobby on this existing atrium, the renovation left it in place but directed guests' attention elsewhere. Filled with plants, the atrium brings natural light to all floors of the hotel, but is not its symbolic center. Before the renovation, the atrium had several colors and contrasting railings (left). The entire space was painted out white in the renovation to make it more harmonious with the traditional flavor of the hotel.
Pre-renovation photo by Kimpton Hotel and Restaurant Group, Inc. Renovation photograph by John Vaughn.

Rosenblatt used Roman shades and draw drapes to frame the windows more conventionally while allowing their exterior appearance to remain the same.

On the guest room floors, the constraints of the building and the Kimpton quest to avoid the ordinary added up to what Rosenblatt called "three hotels in one." At the top floor, the existing greenhouse windows were left in place, and nine special "Starlight" rooms were designed to fit under them. Although the rooms are no larger than the standard ones on lower floors, the dramatic sloping glass which forms most of their exterior walls gives them the atmosphere of a penthouse or a skybox. Kimpton also created nine "townhouse" suites, each two stories high with a private stair. There is a living room and powder room on the lower level and a bedroom and bath on the upper floor. The floors containing the "Starlight" and "Townhouse" accommodations are fitted out as "concierge levels," with their own living room, wine tastings, and concierge service.

Like all Kimpton hotels, the property includes a restaurant with its own identity which is operated separately from the hotel. As it commonly does, Kimpton Group hired a different designer for the restaurant, and later hired a high-profile executive chef to launch the operation. Designer Ron Leiberman gave Pazzo Ristorante a wine cellar theme, with large wood shelves along the perimeter displaying the wine stock, topped by ornamental glass and ceramic wine jugs and bottles. A pyramid of wood fermenting casks and hams hanging to cure add to the theme. Shallow arches in the ceiling suggest a stone structure, while earth tone colors and area rugs build on the informal flavor with a touch of the rustic.

MAKE YOURSELF AT HOME
A Kimpton trademark is "living rooms" instead of lounges and lobbies, with informal furniture intended to coax guests into using the spaces to relax. As an added incentive, the operator serves wine each afternoon in this club level lounge.
Photograph by John Vaughn.

GETTING DOWN TO BUSINESS
In addition to appealing to the boutique market, the Vintage Plaza includes seven meeting rooms to accommodate conventional hotel business. This board room is one of two in the property.
Photograph by John Vaughn.

GUTTED TWICE
Although the building was originally a hotel, it was gutted and partially rehabbed as speculative office space, but never occupied, before the renovation began.
Photograph by Kimpton Hotel and Restaurant Group, Inc.

HOUSE VINTAGE
Standard room sizes and shapes vary as dictated by the building configuration. Color themes are based on hunter green, deep plum, cerise, taupe and gold, with rope medallion patterned fabric. They include granite night stands and chests, honor bar and refrigerator, hair dryers, daily newspaper and free shoe shine.
Photograph by John Vaughn.

AERIE VARIATION
Existing greenhouse windows at the perimeter of the top floor inspired the "Starlight" rooms, with light paints and fabrics, white case goods and rattan furniture. The rooms have deluxe baths with whirlpool tubs.
Photograph by John Vaughn.

UPSTAIRS DOWNSTAIRS
The two-story "Townhouse" suites have the same case goods as the standard rooms, but the rest of their design is special. To develop the winery theme, colors are based on chardonnay grapes, cabernet grapes on a black ground and burgundy. The suites, which feature a sitting room (bottom) with stairs up to a bedroom (top), also have more accessories than the standard rooms.
Photographs by John Vaughn.

The Governor Hotel
Portland, Oregon

The lobby of the Governor Hotel features a
huge mural commissioned for the renovation,
picturing the early 19th century expedition of
Lewis and Clark through uncharted wonders
of North America. The voyage of the hotel
property from its beginning 100 years after
Lewis and Clark up to the 1992 renovation
was similar in some ways, and almost as
exotic. It started with two luxurious buildings
in the early 20th century, led to decline so bad
one of the buildings was used as the location
for an abandoned building scene in a movie,
and culminated with a one-year-long renovation creating a luxury property.

HISTORICAL FIGURES
*Some of the figures in the lobby mural are larger than
life-size; scenes depict sites throughout the state. The
mural painter retraced the Lewis andClark route
through Oregon to research sites, fauna and flora and
historic clothing and tools. She also traveled to New
York to study the palette used in a 1930s Works Progress
Administration-style mural in Rockefeller Center.*
Photograph by Langdon Clay.

Name	**The Governor Hotel**
Location	**Portland, Oregon**
Owner	**The Governor Hotel Associates**
Operator	**Salishan Lodge**
Type of Hotel	**Luxury**
Date of Original Construction	**1909**
Number of Rooms	**100**
Bars & Restaurants	**One each**
Meeting Rooms (Number & Size)	**9 / 14,000 square feet**
Recreation Facilities	**Exercise machines, lap pool, indoor track, steam room, whirlpool**
Type of Renovation	**Hotel shut down during renovation**
Cost	**$15 million**
Date	**1991-1992**
Architect	**Stastny & Burke; Architecture, Portland, Oregon**
Interior Designer	**Candra Scott and Associates, San Francisco, California**
Consultants	**Historic Consultant: Heritage Investment Corp., Portland, Oregon Kitchen Consultant: Allan King and Friends, Reno, Nevada Structural Engineer: KPFF, Portland, Oregon**
Contractor	**P & C Construction Co., Gresham, Oregon**
Masonry Restoration	**Pioneer Waterproofing Company, Portland, Oregon**

ALL ROADS LEAD TO OREGON
*The design of the lobby is pure Oregon, but the sources cover a lot more
territory. The carpet was custom made in England to match the original one
found in the hotel, with the pattern enlarged and the colors changed to the
palette used in the renovation. The 60-foot mural depicting the expedition of
Lewis and Clark was painted on canvas in California by artist Melinda Morey.
The pendant light fixtures, originally from a hotel in Los Angeles, came from a
New York salvage dealer. The round table in the foreground was custom made
for the project; its surface is a radial-keyed veneer designed to look like the
end-grain of a log; the drawer faces are studded leather and the pulls are hand
made metal birds' heads.*
Photograph by Langdon Clay.

FREQUENT GUEST
The standard wall sconce for the renovation was based on an art deco original that interior designer Candra Scott obtained from a San Francisco lighting fixture company. She had the face cast for reproduction, added the mica headdress panels, and applied a faux-bronze finish.
Photograph by Langdon Clay.

FAMILIAR FACE
The Indian head relief on each side of the fireplace was inspired by the custom wall sconces made for the renovation project. The image is not original to the hotel, but its repetition unifies the interior and emphasizes the made-to-order character of the interior.
Photograph by Langdon Clay.

BAR MIX
The bar illustrates the eclectic sources of the hotel interior and the predominant color theme of the public spaces. The focal photograph behind the bar shows an American Indian dancing in front of a Chinese dragon; this cultural match continues in the hotel's signature Indian head wall sconces and the backlit Chinese ceramic grilles under the bar.
Photograph by Langdon Clay.

The Governor Hotel, originally known as the Seward Hotel, was built in 1909 following a tourist boom in Portland set off by the 1905 Lewis and Clark Exposition. Designed by William C. Knighton, a local architect who was appointed State Architect by Governor Oswald West, the gray terra cotta building is ornamented with blue and off-white relief blocks in elaborate anthropomorphic forms which appear to synthesize contemporary European and Pre-Columbian motifs. The renovated hotel is far larger than the original structure, thanks to the annexation of the adjacent historic Princeton Building, which was constructed as the Portland Elks Temple, modeled after the Renaissance architectural monument Palazzo Farnese in Rome. The original Seward-Governor building is now known as the west wing and the Princeton Building is called the east wing.

Connected on the ground floor only, the two buildings are different in function and style. The renovation project originally involved only the Governor Building, but an unfortunate delay in financing the project had the fortunate effect of adding the Princeton Building to the

KEEPING UP APPEARANCES
The renovation included dramatic lighting for the exterior of the building, along with restoration of some of the ground floor store fronts, which had been removed during the property's earlier decline. Exterior improvements also included removal of metal fire escapes, cleaning brick and terra cotta, restoring the entry canopy and installing new awnings.
Photograph by Langdon Clay.

project after design was already under way. The designers linked the buildings, but did not try to make them look or function as if they had always been united. The meeting and banquet space is concentrated in the east wing and the lobby and most of the guest rooms are in the west wing.

Although both are listed on the National Register of Historic Places, the west wing is a vernacular interpretation of the Vienna Secessionist movement while the east wing is by-the-book Renaissance. The east wing is an

American social palace typical of its early 1920s era, with ceilings as high as 33 feet, an 80-foot long banquet hall with white and gold Sienna marble, marble columns and huge fireplaces. Largely intact, it posed no design quandry to the renovation team, which limited changes to restoration tasks like replacing damaged paint and plaster.

The west wing was in relatively good condition on the exterior, but the interior was outmoded, deteriorated and, because of previous retail conversions, very disjointed. The upper floors were to be

gutted and the ground floor reconfigured, leaving the interior a bare armature. To flesh it out with a distinct character and personality, interior designer Candra Scott of San Francisco studied the original design of the hotel and the history and wildlife of her native Oregon. Instead of bright colors and a formal look, she chose a palette based on autumnal Oregon with rich, warm golds, persimmons and greens. Some elements of the original design, such as the signature geometric bell-motif medallion and the carpet pattern, were replicated with little or no change. Where research uncovered designs unappealing to

NEW DINING VENUE
The new restaurant occupies the former location of the lobby. The space retains its original mahogany paneling, casework and ceiling, all stripped and refinished (left). Ground floor public spaces were reconfigured extensively for retail use and natural wood detailing was painted out after the hotel's decline in the Great Depression (bottom).
Before photograph by Stastny and Burke; renovation photograph by John Hughel.

eyes of today's market — there were only rocking chairs in the original lobby — Scott added her own intentionally eclectic mix of Oregon vernacular, Craftsman, chinoiserie, Adirondack, Native American, and demolition salvage.

On the ground floor, the mahogany-paneled lobby with a wood-burning fireplace looks like as if it had been sympathetically reworked during the renovation, but it is actually a newly created space. The original lobby is now the restaurant. Guest room floors, although completely gutted and reconfigured, respect the location of the original windows (many of which were restored) and include fireplaces in many rooms, even though the original hotel did not have them. The entire west wing has all-new building systems and elevators.

The top two floors of the east wing, which were gutted and marketed unsuccessfully as speculative office space in the 1985 renovation of that building, were re-gutted and renovated as guest room floors along with the upper stories of the west wing. The remaining floors of the east wing, originally the social function rooms of the Elks Temple, were restored for use as meeting rooms. Both buildings needed a seismic upgrade, which was straightforward in the gutted west wing but required extra design effort in the east wing, where historic interiors could not easily be disturbed for structural work.

ROOM FOR CHANGE
The original guest rooms were not grandiose by today's standards — many did not have private baths. Years of economic decline added a thick layer of shabbiness to the spartan base by the time of the renovation, which started with full interior demolition (below). The color palettes in the new guest rooms are a lighter version of the lobby colors, wheat, sage, and soft browns. The casings and moldings replicate the original ones in the building.
Before photograph by Stastny & Burke; renovation photograph by Langdon Clay.

IN THE HALLWAYS OF POWER AND PRESTIGE
When it opened in the 1920s, the Elks Temple was designed to give Portland a meeting place worthy of Europe's aristocracy. The grand spaces, restored in 1985 and touched up again in 1992, are now available as hotel meeting space. Each room has a distinct style and special materials (clockwise from bottom left): the ballroom ceiling has caricatures of Elks Club personalities painted in and between the lunettes; a typical hallway leading to the meeting rooms has a two-color marble floor and a barrel-vaulted ceiling with ornate detail; another meeting room features elaborate classical columns; and the rich wood shelves, paneling and coffered ceiling remain in the former library.
Bottom left photograph by Langdon Clay, others by John Hughel.

PARTY CRASHER
Business displaces pleasure where a ballroom was converted to office space. The original Elks Temple had six floors, most of them double-height social spaces. This floor, originally a ballroom, was converted for office use in the 1980s with the insertion of a two-story office pavilion, which was retained in the 1992 hotel renovation as the hotel business center. Merry-makers need not worry: most of the other gathering spaces of the original Elks Temple were retained as meeting and banquet rooms.
Photograph by John Hughel.

The St. Regis
New York, New York

John Jacob Astor commissioned New York architects Trowbridge and Livingston to make his St. Regis Hotel the ultimate statement of European opulence and classical design. By contemporary accounts, his beaux-arts property on Fifth Avenue met that goal when it opened in 1904. An addition in 1927 made the great hotel larger, but not necessarily grander, and subsequent renovations only left the marks of time, not a classical patina, on the building. At the top of New York's hotel market, past glory is a plus, but perfection in the present is must.

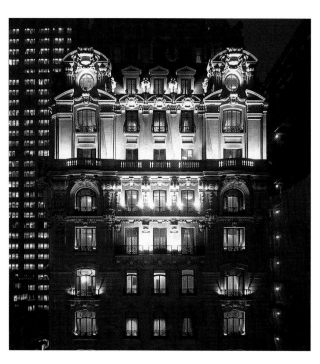

BRIGHT NEW FACE ON A BELOVED LANDMARK
Exterior changes were minimal, stressing repair and preservation of the building, which is a New York City landmark. Dramatic new exterior lighting showcases the termination of the limestone-clad beaux-arts facade. Fixtures had to be carefully concealed on balconies and other unobtrusive locations. The St. Regis towered above its neighborhood when it was completed in 1904, but at eighteen stories it is dwarfed by today's Manhattan hotels.
Photograph by Anthony P. Albarello.

Name	**The St. Regis**
Location	**New York, New York**
Owner	**ITT Sheraton Corporation**
Operator	**ITT Sheraton Corporation**
Type of Hotel	**Luxury**
Date of Original Construction	**1904 / Wing Added 1927**
Number of Rooms	**313**
Bars & Restaurants	**Astor Court**
	King Cole Bar and Lounge
	Lespinasse
Meeting Rooms (Number & Size)	**20 / 15,185 square feet**
Recreation Facilities	**Exercise machines, massage room, sauna**
Type of Renovation	**Gutting and interior reconstruction**
	Hotel shut down for 3 years
Cost	**$100 million-plus**
Date	**Fall 1988 - September 1991**
Architect	**Brennan Beer Gorman Monk / Architects, New York**
Interior Design	**Brennan Beer Gorman Monk / Interiors, New York**
	Graham Design, Woburn, Massachusetts
	ITT Sheraton Corp.
Consultants	**Structural Engineer: DeSimone, Chaplin & Dobryn Consulting Engineers**
	Mechanical Engineer: Flack & Kurtz Consulting Engineers
	Lighting: Theo Kondos Associates
Contractor	**Tishman Construction Co., Inc.**

SEEKING A CENTER
*The strengthened organization of the public spaces on the ground floor
of the 1927 wing pivots around a new public space, the Astor Court,
which connects the King Cole Bar, the Lespinasse restaurant, and the
new entry lobby. Marble columns and gilded composite-order Roman
capitals and entablature, a trompe-l'oeil painted sky on the ceiling, and
a classical Maria Theresa crystal and bronze chandelier make the space
grand, but the effect is not harsh, thanks to the soft, creamy tone of the
painted plaster surfaces and the marble flooring. The original hotel's
design is recalled in varietal furniture with strains of French 19th-
century beaux-arts and Louis XVI styles.*
Photograph by Anthony P. Albarello.

CLEAR ILLUSION
*The new Astor Court is intended to
recreate the spirit of the great art
glass ceiling which the original 1904
hotel contained but lost years before
the renovation. Classical columns
with mythical-looking paintings in
the entablature frieze and a crystal
chandelier suggest the glory of
yesteryear in a space which was
actually created only yesterday.*
Photograph by Anthony P. Albarello.

ELEGANCE AT EASE
In the Cognac Room between the reception lobby and new entry lobby, designers restored the original marble fireplace, mahogany paneling, gold leaf plaster moldings and vaulted ceiling, adding silk damask draperies to create a palatial atmosphere worthy of a robber baron. French chairs and sofa with tapestry-patterned upholstery reinforce the richness but soften the formality of the space enough to encourage late 20th-century guests to make themselves at home.
Photograph by Anthony P. Albarello.

ARTISTIC SPIRITS
"Old King Cole" painted by Maxfield Parrish in 1906 had been a resident at the St. Regis since 1935, reigning over the main restaurant and bar before the renovation. Creation of the more formal Lespinasse restaurant called for a separate space for the painting, which had originally hung in the bar at the Knickerbocker Hotel. The new King Cole Bar is located in what was a service and retail area before the renovation. The 8 foot by 29 foot mural dominates the bar. Visible through glass doors to Astor Court, it serves as the visual terminus of the new spatial axis of the ground floor. Cherrywood paneling and fabric and carpet colors reinforce the warm hues in the painting, while Tuscan pilasters next to the mural mirror those inside it. Simplified but exaggerated molding profiles strengthen the masculine flavor of the space and stand out in the intimate penumbra which contrasts with the strong lighting on the painting.
Photograph by Anthony P. Albarello.

WELCOME CHANGE
*Where the florist shop existed before the renovation, a
new entrance from 55th Street with marble flooring, a
French console and elaborate torchieres gives the ground
floor an opulent sense of spaciousness. The floral fabrics
and plush upholstery in the adjacent sitting area soften
the formality enough to make mortal guests linger.*
Photographs by Anthony P. Albarello.

ITT Sheraton, which had operated the hotel since 1966 and became owner in 1988, vowed to regain Astor's vision when it retained Brennan Beer Gorman / Architects and Brennan Beer Gorman Monk / Interiors of New York as renovation designers in 1988. The key, according to Gustin Tan, project manager for interior architecture, was to embody "the good, old tradition, so it would never go out of fashion," avoiding like the plague any touches which would prompt guests in 1998 to see a "1980s look" in the property.

Interestingly, if Astor were alive today, he would barely recognize the interior of the hotel, despite the praise of guests and critics who think it has been carefully restored to its original condition. Except

for parts of the first two floors, the whole building was gutted and reconfigured. Guest rooms grew in size and shrank in number from 557 to 313, circulation and building systems improved and a host of odd construction configurations and design statements which had accumulated over the years disappeared.

Old friends who swear the building hasn't changed can be forgiven: the renovation did restore some of the most significant spaces without changing them much. The lobby and second floor meeting rooms in the original part of the building were restored, and the ambience of the famous St. Regis Roof ballroom and the barber shop, two other features dear to New

Yorkers, were carefully preserved, while the rest of the building was recreated in its original spirit, if not in its exact image.

The renovation replaced three ground floor retail slots with a new entry and sitting area, tying these and adjacent reconfigured bar and restaurant spaces into a unified order with a new double-height court. The new space, Astor Court, was intended to evoke the original hotel's famous Palm Court. The original court's stained-glass ceiling had a Belle Époque air of Paris, while the new one suggests a more 17th-century France, with classical marble columns, gilded capitals, and a trompe-l'oeil painted sky on the ceiling.

ATTENTION TO DETAILS
Restoration of the lobby included preservation of the details like the ornate revolving door (left) which gave the hotel its original beaux-arts appeal when it opened in 1904. The brass letter box and mail chute (above) have outlived the four-cent stamp, and will undoubtedly survive longer than the 32-cent version after their restoration.
Photographs by Anthony P. Albarello.

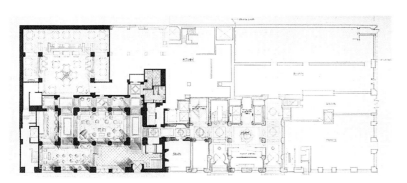

SUBTLE CHANGES
*Slight rearrangements in the lobby,
such as moving the concierge desk,
required major effort. The architect
traveled three times to Italy to
match the existing floor marble in
areas exposed for the first time
because of changes.*
Photographs by Anthony P. Albarello.

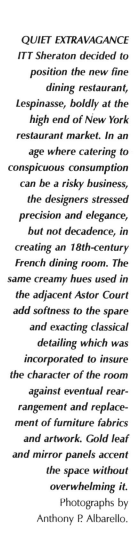

New meeting rooms on the second floor of the 1927 wing are grouped around a double-height pre-function area created by removing a mezzanine slab. The corridors on guest room floors were moved to allow five-fixture bathrooms to be located uniformly on the hallway side of the rooms, with each element in the rooms laid out with classical balance and order to make the design look "as inevitable as possible," according to Tan.

In addition to all-new back-of-the-house areas, the project incorporated new circulation features even where the original design did not change. Two new elevators take guests from the lobby directly to the St. Regis Roof ballroom, keeping them out of the four guest room floor elevators, which handled all upper floors before the renovation. Handicapped accessibility was achieved through installation of wheelchair lifts between areas on different levels within a single floor, because ramps were not compatible with the style of the building. The new large express elevators to the ballroom stop on guest room floors when activated by a key for the handicapped.

ADDED CACHET
The Fontainbleau Suite in the 1927 wing is a completely new room, created by demolition of a mezzanine above the second floor level to allow a double-height ceiling. Plaster moldings, gold leaf and chandeliers and sconces (detail, right) similar to the ones in the original 1904 ballrooms made the new meeting rooms so successful after the reopening that unfinished space in the basement was later reconfigured to create two more new suites, the Maisonette and the Iridium.
Photographs by Anthony P. Albarello.

BREAKFAST AT TIFFANY'S
The renovated hotel features three unique specialty suites, one designed by Christian Dior, and another by John Loring, design director of Tiffany & Co. The dining room of the suite Loring designed is inspired by London clubs of the era of the construction of the St. Regis. The hotel's other suites proved so popular after the reopening that alterations have been undertaken to convert regular corner guest rooms on each floor into suites.
Photograph by Anthony P. Albarello.

HEIGHT OF ELEGANCE
The St. Regis Roof ballroom, located at the top of the building and near the top of New York Society's food chain, was subtly reworked as part of the renovation. The cloud-painted ceiling replaces an earlier solid-color canopy; the French curves of the cove around the ceiling hide ventilation and other utilitarian gear. While restraint was the watchword in decorating lower public spaces, extravagance was the order of the day in the ballroom, with lavish draperies, applied decoration, painted vaults, and crystal chandeliers.
Photograph by
Anthony P. Albarello.

weren't even hotel luxuries when the century began but have become necessities as it comes to an end: a business center and a fitness center. Both are located on the new "lower level" in what used to be the basement, which has been upgraded with new circulation spaces, the barber shop, and two meeting rooms. The business center has office machines, a reception area and a private office for guests. The nearby fitness center includes a good-sized room with exercise machines, a massage room, a sauna and changing rooms.

SLIGHT CHANGE OF VENUE
The Versailles Ballroom (abowe) and the Louis XVI Suite (left) were not gutted during the renovation. The popular reception spaces on the second floor of the original 1904 section of the building did receive new mechanical, audio-visual and life-safety systems along with a complete refurbishment of their finishes.
Photographs by Anthony P. Albarello.

CLASSICAL COMPOSITION

Guest rooms have tie-back draperies, Louis XV and Louis XVI furniture, crystal chandeliers, and painstaking coordination of architecture, fixtures and furniture. If the basic elements of 18th century millwork are interpreted with strength and simplicity, "then a room will at least have 'good bones' and shouldn't need gilded spaghetti to make it look elegant," according to designer Jinnie Kim of Graham Design. Room features are coordinated so that guests don't enter on the sidewall of a room or look up from their beds at the edge of a sofa. Color schemes are based on palettes of muted blue or green, silver and blue, or ruby red.
Photographs by Anthony P. Albarello.

MARBLE, MARBLE EVERYWHERE

All bathrooms have five fixtures, including two sinks in a marble countertop, a tub with marble surround, a toilet room, and a separate shower stall. When ITT Sheraton opted for the bathroom upgrade during the design process, architects had to go back to their drawing boards and gut all guest room floors and move corridors to accommodate the change.
Photographs by Anthony P. Albarello.

The Broadway American Hotel

New York, New York

When the years have blurred the appeal of an old building into grime-covered blandness, a limited-budget renovation design might reconfigure the most outmoded rooms or floors to current standards, replace the most damaged systems and building fabric, and then refinish everything in a fresh but not too daring style. New York architect Manuel Castedo took a very different tack in renovating a twelve-story hotel on Manhattan's West Side. He inserted eye-catching new walls and ceilings to reconfigure major public spaces, leaving cut-outs to expose remnants of the original building and its plaster detailing. The new elements are figural, rectilinear and graphic, an intentional contrast with the old. And eschewing the conventional approach of treating the whole building uniformly, the renovation team left guest-room floor layouts intact, allowing a higher budget for public spaces and items which see a lot of wear.

FINER THINGS
The decision to retain guest room floor layouts allowed the renovation designers to devote more money to areas guests see most, such as these service counters in the outer lobby.
Photograph by Ashod Kassabian.

Name	**The Broadway American Hotel**
Location	**New York, New York**
Owner	**Benjamin Franklin Associates**
Operator	**Benjamin Franklin Associates**
Type of Hotel	**European-style Economy**
Date of Original Construction	**1919**
Number of Rooms	**400**
Bars & Restaurants	**None**
Meeting Rooms (Number & Size)	**None**
Recreation Facilities	**None**
Type of Renovation	**Phased, hotel open during construction**
Cost	**$10 million**
Date	**1990-1992**
Architect	**M. Castedo Architect, New York**
Interior Designer	**M. Castedo Architect, New York**
Consultants	**Mechanical, Electrical and Plumbing Engineers: Peter Franzese and John Taylor, New York**
Construction Manager	**TFC Associates, New York**

The building, originally constructed as a luxury apartment house, had been converted to a single room occupancy hotel many years before the renovation, leaving only scattered traces of its grand beginnings. There were ten different guest room configurations, some without private baths. The team decided not to pitch the property at the standard hotel market, but to gear it instead to foreign travelers willing to trade the amenities of mainstream digs for something with an offbeat flavor—and low rates. That created crucial room within the construction budget, which was already tight because of exterior work, new high-speed elevators, and replacement of plumbing and electrical systems.

The ground floor was reconfigured completely, with new interiors which belie the budget limitations. Floors in the entry area are honed granite, woodwork is American cherry, and original artwork was commissioned from a New York artist for the project. The interior design bears out the hotel's name by emphasizing its American character to give foreign guests something they don't get in other countries—or at other hotels.

OUTWARD SIGNS
Changes to the brick and limestone exterior of the building were relatively limited. New store fronts and awnings spruced up ground floor commercial space (above). At the hotel entrance, a simple canopy was added to the existing black granite entry. Despite this restrained design, even passersby get a hint of the new interior when they see the star-spangled wood podium and backlit glass wall behind it (left).
Photographs by Ashod Kassabian.

On the guest room floors, the renovation team put its efforts and budget into making rooms attractive and durable. All guest room furniture was custom designed, with emphasis on daring and enduring construction. Bathroom walls are tiled and the ceiling and fixtures are heavy-duty; bedspreads are custom made by an elevator protection pad manufacturer, and wall paint is crisp-looking Zolatone multicolor splatter, which also happens to hide dirt and wear better than a solid color.

Castedo said his design goal was to promote New York and the Broadway American in a playful manner. It's impossible to predict guests' senses of humor or their reaction to the entire city, but it seems a fair bet that they will remember this hotel as different from the rest.

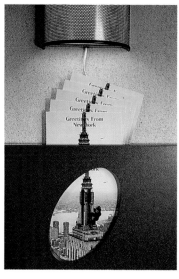

BEDTIME COMPANION
Renovated guest rooms have soft uplighting and blue and gray color schemes to soothe guests after experiencing the stimulating lobby and city outside. Those seeking excitement need look only as far as the cutouts in the custom headboards. Greeting them from this vantage point is none other than King Kong. Postcards of his visit to the Empire State Building are displayed for guests' use, aimed at promoting the hotel and New York in a lighthearted way.
Photograph by Ashod Kassabian.

LAYERS OF EXPOSURE
Although the renovation reconfigured ground floor spaces, it did not eliminate all traces of the original design. Large figural openings in the new ceiling reveal the original ceiling and double as indirect lighting sources. (view from opposite ends of lobby, below left and right). The back-lit glass wall grid brightens the space the way windows onto a courtyard would; guests who take a closer look at the small glass hemispheres in the wall panels find they are windows which reveal photographs of New York landmarks like the Empire State Building (top, left). The colors and pattern of the painting at one end of the lobby reappear in the carpet layout.
Photographs by Ashod Kassabian.

Essex House
New York, New York

"Everything You Remember. And More," was the promise Japan Air Lines subsidiary Nikko Hotels International gave New Yorkers when it bought the Essex House from Marriott in 1985 and launched a major renovation. The new owners hired interior designer Pierre Yves Rochon of Paris and architects Brennan Beer Gorman of New York, instructing them to recreate the spirit of the original 1931 hotel rather than replicate it to the letter. Once a landmark of 1930s design and a major venue of the New York entertainment world, the Essex House had lost its focus over the years, becoming an architectural muddle and a slightly dimmed star in the constellation of New York hotels.

ART DECO IMAGE

The original design of the Essex House was an Art Deco composition visually characteristic of New York between World War I and II. The renovation capitalized on the image of the original exterior of the building as a towering advertisement of the hotel's prestige in New York's history. The exterior received a cleaning, the details were regilded, a new entrance marquise compatible with the rest of the exterior was installed, and dramatic lighting increased the effect at night. The building has a prime location at the foot of Central Park, and is a familiar monument on the skyline

Photographs: (facing page, top) by Peter Vitale, above by Maury Englander.

Name	Essex House Hotel Nikko New York
Location	New York, New York
Owner	Nikko Hotels International
Operator	Nikko Hotels (USA)
Type of Hotel	Luxury
Date of Original Construction	1931
Number of Rooms & Suites	595
Bars & Restaurants	1 bar / 2 restaurants
Meeting Rooms (Number & Size)	8 / 11,211 square feet
Recreation Facilities	Exercise machines, freeweights, steam room, footbath room, sauna, "therapy" showers, locker rooms, health and beauty treatment rooms
Type of Renovation	Hotel closed, complete interior renovation
Cost	$175 million
Date	January 1990 - October 1991
Architect	Brennan Beer Gorman, New York
Interior Designer	Pierre Yves Rochon, Paris
Construction Manager	Tishman Construction, New York

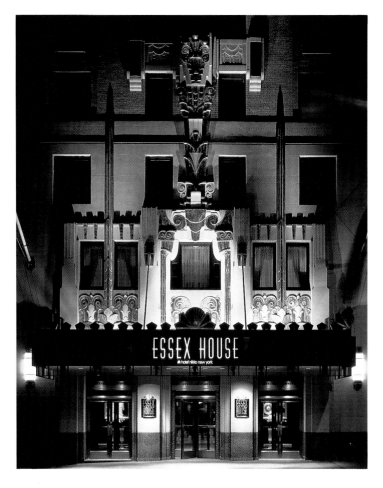

*DON'T ASK ITS AGE
The new lobby looks like a
restoration of the
"original" Art Deco space,
although in fact only the
hand-crafted bronze
elevator doors are
original. Square black
marble columns with Deco
fluting (right rear corner),
etched glass and metal
consoles and grilles look
like restorations of original
elements from the 1930s,
while furniture, lamps,
objets d'art and a pair of
Gatsby-style paintings
cover a wider, more
ambiguous, range
suggesting an Art Deco
space which has been
carefully seasoned to
maturity over the decades.*
Photograph by Peter Vitale.

NO HO-HUM HOTEL RESTAURANT
Les Celebrités, the 55-seat fine dining restaurant created in the renovation, is not a reworking of an original operation, it is a total original in itself.
Photograph by Peter Vitale.

ROUND TRIP
Before the renovation, the lobby of the Essex House had an English club look, adjoined by a nautical-theme bar and restaurant. The renovation changed the image of the lobby and eliminated the adjoining bar, but the English club look survived in the new Journeys bar, which adjoins the back of the three-meal restaurant. Hunting prints hang on the dark wood walls, large leather chairs and couches seem to be waiting for eccentric gentry to sit and read the London Times, and the fireplace boasts a real wood fire in this very warm, but not-too-cozy space.
Photograph by Peter Vitale.

The renovation team redesigned ground floor spaces to bring back the rich, but not decadent, look the hotel had in the 1930s, and reconfigured them to make them more functional and generous. The existing lobby bar was replaced by a seating area, which made room for new windows, opening the view to Central Park across the street. The registration desk was moved, a new concierge desk was added, and a special lobby for the 148 condominium apartments in the hotel replaced the existing business center.

The lobby renovation interprets the hotel's signature Art Deco theme with enough ambiguity to create the impression of an original space which has evolved over time. The main corridor connecting the lobby with the secondary hotel entrance further softens the Art Deco theme, striking a more classical tone with dark-stained casework and paneling. A similar corridor bisects the main one at right angles, connecting the bar and the ballroom and adding a sense of classical organization as well as convenient circulation.

Tucked almost invisibly off this corridor lies the boldest design and marketing venture of the renovation, the Les Celebrités fine dining restaurant. Some other restaurants in the Nikko chain have the same name, but it's safe to say no restaurant in the world has the same interior. Its Lalique centerpieces, Frette linen, Bernardaud china, Christophle silver, Schott Zwiesel crystal, and Italian marble columns may not be strictly unique, and perhaps the rich red walls in the reception salon, dramatic lighting throughout and bold, luxurious fabrics

FRENCH GARDEN
At the front of the Cafe Botanica, the renovation designers had no trouble creating the garden atmosphere they had in mind for the main restaurant: Central Park was across the street, so they increased fenestration and complemented the verdant view with rattan and wicker furniture, floral pattern fabrics, and a palette of green, terra cotta and beige. At the rear of the restaurant, the windows on Central Park are too far away to make much of an impression, so designers created a private French garden with large plants, a stone fountain and a painted "sky" ceiling, enclosed in metalwork custom-fabricated in France.
Photograph by Peter Vitale.

have parallels elsewhere, but this space is definitely one of a kind thanks to its piéce de resistance: celebrity art. Not paintings of celebrities or collected by them — paintings by celebrities. Although the restaurant seats only 55, it attracted plenty of attention from critics, who weighed its merits pronounced it a success in food and design, making reservations almost as hard to get as invitations to celebrity parties.

Cafe Botanica, the property's larger, three-meal-day restaurant, occupies the same space the main restaurant had before the renovation. It has a garden theme with light colors, flower-patterned carpeting, fabrics and table settings, and an airy, open layout. The renovation included the addition of windows to make the space seem like an extension of Central Park across the street and a small palm court at the rear, with a partially-glazed metalwork enclosure, a replica of an original the designers found in a small town in France. Faster than the TGV through the channel tunnel, hotel guests can go from the French palm court to a very proper British setting just by walking through the door to the Journeys Bar. Another example of the non-literal interpretation of the "original" Essex House, this bar picks up the theme of the Bombay Bicycle Club bar in the original hotel. Bits of the original plaster ceiling remained and were replicated during the renovation, but the rest of the design is new.

The renovated ballroom takes guests back to France again, with sparkling new Renaissance pilasters, gilding, white walls with panel molding, frescoes and hand-crafted French chandeliers, all inspired by Versailles and introduced during the renovation. The original two-tier Colon-nade Room, famous decades ago as a venue for the Big Band Sound, had been made one level by the 1960s; and was later

ELEGANT PAUSING PLACE
The elevator lobbies on guest room floors have murals copied from a painting at The Metro-politan Museum of Art. Custom-pattern carpeting throughout the building was imported from France and Italy.
Photograph by Peter Vitale.

SUITE SUCCESS
The living room of a renovated suite makes its impact with generous wall and ceiling moldings, plenty of traditional furniture and strong, confident carpet and fabric colors and patterns (bottom). Pre-renovation rooms made an impact with lurid carpet colors, hyperactive fabric designs and a smorgasbord of furniture reminiscent of discount stores (top and center).
Photograph (bottom) by Peter Vitale.

redone in generic modern style with gray and maroon tones.

The new business center on the second floor features three private offices as well as the standard machines and services. The renovation also included new heating and air-conditioning systems, new elevators and all new kitchens.

On the guest-room floors, the renovation reduced the room count from 711 to 595 while increasing the number of suites and replaced the chain-hotel-style interiors with 12 different designs and 120 room configurations. Within that variety, there are unifying constants: furniture is Louis XVI in all rooms on the Central Park side of the building and Chippendale on the other side. In all permutations, understated art balances rich wall colors and striking custom fabrics. The goal for guest room renovations was to make guests feel as if they were staying at a friend's house. This "friend" has no financial problems, judging by the custom carpets and marble bathrooms, the VCR, three two-line speaker telephones with data port, electronically-locked safe, individual climate control and mini-bar in each room and the robes, scales, hand-held hair dryers and television speakers in each bathroom. Considering the historic reputation and clientele of the Essex House, such opulence isn't too much of a surprise — in fact, it might simply be described as "Everything You Remember. And More."

VIEW WITH A ROOM
The north side of the hotel looks out on Central Park, giving guests a view which can't be beat in New York. Before the renovation, the thick-pile carpeting in saturated colors, plaid wall-covering and medley of furniture and fabrics may have distracted guests who thought they would enjoy the park view (above). Although the renovated guest rooms have strong colors and fabrics and rich Louis XVI furniture, the unity of design and substantial, traditional materials give them a more understated quality
Photograph (facing page) by Peter Vitale.

The Equinox
Manchester, Vermont

No matter how beautiful it is or how significant the events and guests it has seen, even a historic hotel has to fit into the current market, or "it's history," as the expression goes. At the Equinox, one renovation gave new life to the historic building, but the business floundered until a second makeover looked to the marketplace, and repositioned the property as a destination resort.

LONG LINE OF HISTORY
The Equinox began as the Marsh Tavern; the building grew with the business as successive owners added and acquired adjacent structures. The building has had 17 major architectural changes and additions over the years, and exhibits six different styles of architecture. The renovation did not include substantial changes to the rambling front elevation of the hotel which faces the village green.

Name	**The Equinox**
Location	**Manchester, Vermont**
Owner	**Equinox Resort Associates**
Operator	**The Gleneagles Group**
Type of Hotel	**Resort**
Date of Original Construction	**1769**
Number of Rooms	**136, plus 27 in investor-owned townhouses**
Bars & Restaurants	**2 restaurants / 1 bar**
Meeting Rooms Number & Size	**8 rooms / 14,000 square feet**
Recreation Facilities	**18-hole golf course, indoor and outdoor pool, 3 clay tennis courts, spa with health and beauty treatments, free-weights and exercise machines, exercise classes, sauna and steam room**
Type of Renovation	**Phased market reposition, partial hotel shut down**
Cost	**$13 million**
Date	**1991 - 1993; reopened 1992**
Master Renovation Designer	**Tag Galleon**
Architect and Interior Designer	**Ahearn & Shoffner, Boston, Massachusetts**
Contractor	**Albany**

The Equinox began in 1769 as the Marsh Tavern; a few years later it was a meeting place for the Vermont Green Mountain Boys during the American Revolution. In the 19th century, it attracted Mary Todd Lincoln as a summer guest as it grew into a grand, rambling monument of New England architecture set between a village green and two mountain ranges.

By the 1980s, the Equinox was past its prime as a business and nearing the point of no return as a building, prompting a group of concerned Vermonters to jump in and save the hotel with a renovation. Physically preserved, the property still did not find a niche in the hospitality market. In the early 1990s, a group of investors led by operators of the Gleneagles Hotel and Golf Course in Scotland took over and renovated the Equinox again, focusing it as a luxury destination resort.

Their strategy started with an ambitious rebuilding of the property's golf course, upgraded its other recreation facilities, made over the main hotel building, and built a group of upscale shops at the hotel's doorstep. The finished product enabled the operators to market the property as a modern resort with a historic background.

The renovation began with a $3.5 million rebuilding of the 18-hole golf course originally designed by Walter Travis in 1927. Rees Jones rebuilt and upgraded the course, following the original routing and retaining its desirable features. The clubhouse and a fitness center built for the 1985 renovation underwent minor renovations. Rounding out the resort product, the operators coordinated guests'

access to nearby fishing, hunting, riding, hiking, skiing, and canoeing.

Renovating the main hotel building presented a challenge: using a Vermont flavor to differentiate the property from similar resorts elsewhere without turning it into a generic Vermont inn. The solution was to temper the New England look with the substantial feeling of a 150 room resort hotel. Traditional, sober furniture, colors and materials bear out the monumental size and design of the building, while eclectic furniture, including many antiques, look as if they had accumulated over 200 years. Rich, varied fabrics, some of them eccentric, and hints of the local fishing and hunting pursuits create a sense of place. "We wanted it to feel like a really nice sweater," said renovation master designer, Tag Galleon.

OUTDOOR ATTRACTION

The centerpiece of the market reposition was the rebuilding of the golf course on its original routing while moving greens back and recontouring them, rebuilding bunkers, and raising several fairways to improve drainage. The golf course redesign also included a new irrigation system and modern grasses to replace the existing turf.

BOLD REVISION
The Colonnade restaurant interior strikes a bolder and grander note after the renovation (below). The painted stenciling on the ceiling is based on a historic technique and pattern, and gives the room a more detailed appearance than it had before the renovation with its airy solid blue ceiling (right). The draperies, the chandeliers, the red walls, and the green and gold carpet installed in the renovation add to the rich, formal tone of the renovated space.

YOU'VE ARRIVED

The new lobby lets guests know they're at a substantial hotel as soon as they enter the two-story space (below). The furniture is eclectic, but slightly grand and decidedly not rustic or rickety. The rich yellow and white paint scheme sets the tone for the simple, stately Federalist period suggested in the guest room interiors. The previous renovation in the 1980s used velvet and fringe upholstery to create a more Victorian design in the lobby to complement the later style found on the exterior, but the spatial effect was severely limited by the low ceiling in the room (two photographs, left).

The most conspicuous architectural change was moving the lobby, previously located awkwardly at one end of the building, with a ceiling less than eight feet high. To provide an entry with a sense of arrival and convenient circulation, the designers removed existing guest rooms at the center of the structure, creating a new two-story lobby which looks out on the property's courtyard. That freed up the old lobby space for expansion of the Marsh Tavern, the oldest portion of the business.

The rest of the public spaces were all renovated within their existing configurations. Back-of-the-house, the only major change was addition of a small kitchen. Guest-room configurations stayed the same, but bathrooms were gutted and replaced. The existing case goods received new finishes, while the soft goods, architectural finishes and detailing were all replaced.

The renovation took advantage of the need for shopping in a destination resort. The hotel owned buildings on the other side of the village green, and renovated and reconfigured them all for lease as commercial space, later acquiring and renovating additional buildings as business grew. The operators market the renovated property as a year-round resort with a variety of sports and relaxations; a newsletter highlights the activities and special events offered each season and runs features on the businesses around the hotel and their merchandise and services.

NEW FEDERALISM
Guest rooms were revised in a simple, calm design with a touch of the Federal style (above), de-emphasizing the slightly rustic flavor of the existing rooms (right). A fluted picture rail molding was added, a new tweedy carpet replaced the existing one, and case goods were refinished in a bleached natural maple tone.

WHERE IT ALL BEGAN
The hostelry was born as the Marsh Tavern in 1769, and the same space still serves the same function under the same name within the much-evolved Equinox. The renovation which brought the property back from the brink of demolition in the mid-1980s used black and red checkered wall covering to create a homespun, Revolution-period feeling (below). The renovated tavern has a dark green and tan wall covering, a heavy tapestry-like fabric for upholstered furniture, and an assortment of sofas, wingback chairs, and Windsor captain's chairs to provide a more comfortable and substantial environment than the previous collection of all open-wood furniture (right).

Washington Courtyard
Washington, D.C.

One look at the Quality Hotel in Washington, D.C. would probably be enough to make anyone guess why its owner, the Wyoming Hotel Corporation, decided to renovate the property in 1992. With mirrors on the walls and ceiling, the lobby was awash in wavy reflections which looked like the set from a low-budget sci-fi movie about an aquarium gone awry. Guests who ventured further reached a dining room which looked like a tract house interpretation of a medieval dungeon. Not surprisingly, the owner decided that replacing the mostly package-tour clientele with business travelers would require replacing the look of the building as well.

New Name
A year after the renovation, the property switched from a Quality Inn franchise to Courtyard by Marriott. The green awnings, lighted at night to help identify the affiliation, were among the relatively few alterations required by Marriott for the relabeling.

Name	**Washington D.C.Courtyard by Marriott**
Location	**Washington, D.C.**
Owner	**The Wyoming Hotel Corporation**
Operator	**Courtyard by Marriott**
Type of Hotel	**Business / Three Star**
Date of Original Construction	**1968**
Number of Rooms	**148**
Bars & Restaurants	**Bailey's Bar, Claret's Restaurant**
Meeting Rooms (Number & Size)	**2 / 315 square feet each**
Recreation Facilities	**Swimming pool**
Type of Renovation	**Hotel shut down during renovation, fast-track design-build**
Cost	**$5.5 Million**
Date	**March - September 1992**
Architect	**Brennan Beer Gorman / Architects**
Interior Designer	**Brennan Beer Gorman Monk / Interiors**
Consultants	**Structural Engineer: Cagley & Assoc. Mechanical Engineer: JVP Engineers, P.C. Electrical Engineer: Cobb & del Castillo, Ltd.**
Construction Manager	**Coakley & Williams Construction Co., Inc.**

CORRIDORS OF POWER
The renovated lobby (top) and front desk (left) replace the modern minimalist look of the pre-renovation hotel with a dignified traditional appearance. Patterned carpets, tapestry window treatments, and stained casework are topped off by Waterford chandeliers.
Photographs by Dan Cunningham.

After a seven-and-one-half month fast-track renovation carried out under a design-build arrangement with construction manager Coakley & Williams, the property had a completely different atmosphere, a controlled, understated traditional theme. Within a year, the transformation was completed by a switch to the Courtyard by Marriott label.

By focusing the makeover on the most prominent parts of the building, Wyoming, Coakley & Williams and designers at the Washington offices of Brennan Beer Gorman/Architects — Brennan Beer Gorman Monk/Interiors (BBG) effected a major change of image on a limited budget and schedule. Exterior work was concentrated on the ground floor, and changes to interior partitions were limited almost completely to the first floor. Remaining portions of the building received new finishes, but little more. The renovation also included modification of the mechanical system, installation of firesprinklers and life-safety improvements.

Located on the corner of Connecticut Avenue, a commercial thoroughfare, and LeRoy Place, a side street with historic townhouses, the bland building was at odds with its surroundings. It was impossible to blend the massing of the nine-story hotel with the nearby three-

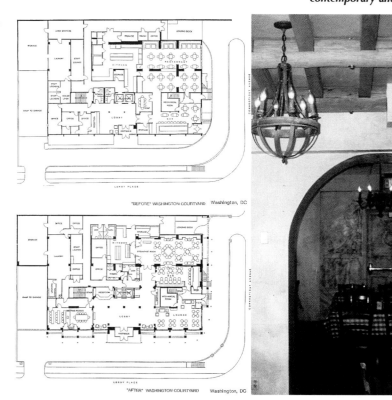

"BEFORE" WASHINGTON COURTYARD   Washington, DC

"AFTER" WASHINGTON COURTYARD   Washington, DC

story townhouses, and the budget did not allow for extensive redesign of the exterior, which Mark Boekenheide, partner-in-charge for BBG described as "a big hulking commercial structure." To alleviate the effect of the size of the building, it was painted a lighter color, and application of synthetic stucco arches at the parapet introduced visual order and a smaller scale.

Most of the exterior budget went into the ground floor, where pedestrians see the

building close-up and get their strongest impression. A large retaining wall at the sidewalk level received a coat of stucco, detailed to imitate cast stone, while a stairway at the street corner was moved to allow more room on the sidewalk. Additional landscaping, lighting, lighted signs, new windows at public areas, and replacement of the store front at the entry rounded out the effort to give the building more identity and pedestrian charm — and win the approval of a neighborhood group and the District's historic review board.

SMART AND BRIGHT
While the lobby and restaurant strike a formal, elite note, Bailey's Bar relaxes a bit with bright but easy-going fabrics, a bold color scheme, and ample downlighting instead of chandeliers.
Photograph by Dan Cunningham.

TOUCH OF CRYSTAL
Claret's Restaurant is smaller than the dining room that existed before the renovation, but it can claim Waterford chandeliers and beveled mirrors.
Photograph by Dan Cunningham.

Interior changes on the ground floor were driven not only by the owner's need for a new look, but by business differences between the package tour and business travel markets. The large restaurant and kitchen shrank to accommodate a more generous lobby and the introduction of meeting rooms. Guests can see the single biggest design change before they enter the ground floor: twelve new windows. "It was like a tomb" with just one window in the lobby before the renovation, Boekenheide said, so the designers tore out an exterior wall and replaced it with glazing "to get some life into the lobby."

Although the renovated first floor spaces share a sense of traditional dignity and warm, rich colors and materials, they vary from the sedate and slightly clubby lobby to the somewhat richer restaurant and the bright and energetic bar. The hotel's Irish ownership explains the lobby and restaurant Waterford chandeliers, which it provided directly to the job. They stand out as the most opulent element in the property, compatible with the style of the rooms, but contrasting with the suspended-grid acoustic system used in the ceilings.

On guest-room floors, crown moldings, striped wall coverings, and increased lighting from new ceiling and wall fixtures provide a general upgrade for circulation areas. Narrow side tables and mirrors in each corridor and half-inch wood moldings applied to the flush guest-room doors help break up the length and monotony that simple, unadorned hallways can have. The budget limit is more evident in the amount of work done on the

LUXURY WITH LIMITS
Bathrooms in the standard guest rooms are compact, leaving too little room for installation of vanities. To make the most of the space, the renovation design provides pedestal sinks with glass shelves above, large mirrors, and 12-inch-square marble tiling on the walls and floors. Marriott usually requires vanities in bathrooms in the Courtyard series, but accepted the space-conscious design for the Washington property.
Photograph by Dan Cunningham.

CAREFULLY MEASURED
Standard rooms carry out the traditional look of the public spaces, but on a more limited budget for materials and details. The television armoire, like other wood case goods, adds a substance to the very simple room — and also saves space by eliminating the need for a dresser.
Photograph by Dan Cunningham.

A CUT ABOVE
The large rooms at the end of each floor of the hotel have one king bed, a writing desk, easy chair with ottoman, and wood base and crown moldings, plus a larger bathroom than the standard rooms.
Photograph by
Dan Cunningham.

INSIDE THE BELTWAY Although they may not get White House invitations, at least VIPs visiting Washington don't have to compete with the President for this fancy hotel room. The Presidential Suite has a living-dining room in addition to the bedroom and bathroom. It follows the theme of other guest rooms in the hotel, but with chandeliers, oriental rugs and higher-grade fabrics. Movers and shakers can relax in an armchair while keeping an eye on the capital scene.
Photographs by
Dan Cunningham.

SUMPTUOUS BATHING
The bathroom in the presidential suite features a whirlpool bath tub and separate shower, marble vanity and built-in hair dryer. Marble on the floors and walls matches that found in other bathrooms in the hotel.
Photograph by Dan Cunningham.

guest rooms, which have less detail but maintain the traditional theme of the ground floor with wood headboards and case goods. Television armoires with dresser drawers conserve space in the rooms. They are arrayed in nine different ways on each floor, none with an excess of space. The rooms at the ends of each floor are enlarged and have wood base and crown moldings, a king-size bed, better finish materials, a writing desk, mini-bar and marble-tiled baths with vanities. Completed in time for the 1993 inauguration, the presidential suite has a living-dining room, all-marble bathroom and bedroom with king-size bed, and a second bedroom with two queen beds and its own bathroom.

Like the design, the renovation process was judiciously calculated to make the most of the owner's investment. Coakley & Williams gave Wyoming a single point of responsibility for design and construction and a fixed price at the outset of the project, and acted as construction manager. BBG had performed a pre-purchase survey for Wyoming and had worked with Coakley & Williams previously, so the design-build team could hit the ground running.

It certainly had to do that, with only seven-and-one-half months for design and construction, and a schedule which called for awarding subcontracts at the 75 percent stage of design for most work.

Wyoming decided to shut the hotel down for construction and steer regular guests to a nearby property it owned, avoiding a longer renovation which might drive some of them away permanently. The renovation was not tailored to the Courtyard by Marriott brand change, but only limited changes, such as landscaping, resurfacing the deck and removing an existing wood bar at the swimming pool; painting the parking garage and adding the chain's signature green awnings, were required when the switch was made a year after the renovation.

Hyatt Regency New Orleans

New Orleans, Louisiana

When the Hyatt Regency New Orleans opened in the mid-1970s, it gave the Crescent City a dose of slick, splashy architecture. Guests arriving at the motor entrance passed through a wall of glass doors into a lobby with a strong spare interior and up a two-story escalator to a 27-story atrium. The tables were turned when the property got its first major renovation in the early 1990s. The designers introduced New Orleans tradition to the perennially new-looking hotel, replacing giant mobiles and mass-produced materials with traditional chandeliers and marble.

STILL LOOKING NEW

The exterior appearance of the hotel did not change during the renovation, despite introduction of a more traditional look on the interior. The 32-story hotel is part of a complex which includes an office building, a convention center, and the Louisiana Superdome.
Photograph by Ken Glaser.

Name	*Hyatt Regency New Orleans*
Location	*New Orleans, Louisiana*
Owner	*Prudential Realty Corporation*
Operator	*Hyatt Hotels Corporations*
Type of Hotel	*Convention*
Date of Original Construction	*1979*
Number of Rooms	*1,384*
Bars & Restaurants	*5*
Meeting Rooms Number & Size	*35 rooms / 90,000 square feet*
Recreation Facilities	*Rooftop swimming pool, health club with exercise machines, weights*
Type of Renovation	*Phased renovation, hotel closed only 2 days*
Cost	*$16 million*
Date	*1992 - 1995*
Architect and Interior Designer	*Public Spaces, Meeting Rooms: Newmark Diercks Design Inc., Greenwood Village, Colorado Regency Club: Gayle Bird Interiors, Ltd., New Orleans, Louisiana Guest Rooms: Rosemont Purchasing, Chicago, Illinois*
Consultants	*Technical Architectural Services: John Hardy Group*
Contractor	*Case & Associates, Houston, Texas*

BEGINNING AND END
The scope of the renovation did not allow replacement of the existing brown brick walls the full height of the
registration lobby, so the designers had to find a location to end the new interior and let the old one continue. They
topped off the new registration, bellman, and concierge desks with illuminated etched glass canopies, framing the
new composition, and upstaging the existing wall, which continues behind it. The new canopies incorporate to
make a subtle reference to traditional New Orleans design without contrasting too much with the contemporary
styling of the hotel. The remodeling also provided a new finish to the same height on the structural columns,
replacing the existing brown brick with mahogany and marble. The new materials are detailed to stress the
verticality of the column and de-emphasize its width.
Photograph by Karl Francetic.

In the lobby, the sleek, open look and consistent, limited range of materials used in the original design were scrutinized by the designers during the renovation. They reduced the amount of brown brick, the original wall and floor finish material, and increased the amount of architectural detail. The designers removed the doors at the center of the store-front construction motor entrance, moved the wall outward, and installed new brass doors to create a stronger sense of arrival and spatial sequence. The redefinition continues inside the lobby, where the new marble flooring is articulated with a band of contrasting colors along the axis from the entry to the main lobby. Materials, detailing, and furniture in the lobby flesh out the more formal, traditional overtone of the renovated interior, recalling classical motifs

subtly to avoid clashing with the contemporary overall style of the building.

Subtle changes were made to the Hyatt's signature - an atrium large enough to house a small skyscraper. The existing tent-like canopies which defined the restaurant and cocktail lounge on the atrium floor gave way to mahogany baldacchino-style structures with a New Orleans character in their detailing and wrought iron railings. In the hotel's Regency Club on the concierge level, a more pronounced transformation of style took place. A spare, modern design was replaced with traditional sofas, armchairs, draperies, and lighting. Substance to accompany the style included a new business center for guests on the upgrade floor, with work areas, office machines, and a video phone.

The meeting space in the hotel is divided in two areas and also underwent a facelift during the renovation. The renovation added a business center and a hotel-operated flower shop to the smaller of the two facilities. At the rooftop pool deck, two existing suites were converted into hospitality suites catering to business and meeting guests. Each has a mini-kitchen, a service bar, a table for conference or dining use, and a seating area. Additional guest room space at the pool deck was converted into a new health club, with stair and cycling exercise machines, weight-lifting machines, and free weights. The renovation also included an overhaul of the restaurant and bars of the hotel.

WELCOME TO THE CLUB
The Regency Club Lounge on the hotel's concierge floor traded in its existing sharp, contemporary design for a traditional look. Comfortable classic furniture, tall floor lamps and conservative art impart a steady, slightly understated air to the room. The suites on the concierge level, which were Chinese modern style before the renovation, also switched to a more traditional look, with wrought iron details and crystal chandeliers.
Photograph by Ken Glaser.

MEET THE NEW MEETING SPACE
The renovation revamped the finishes in each of the meeting rooms. This included: the 25,000 square foot French Market Exhibition Hall (top), the smaller conference center rooms, and the concourse and meeting rooms in the separate Regency Conference Center (bottom), located in an adjoining building connected to the hotel (center).

Photographs by Ken Glaser.

NEW FROM THE GROUND UP
The 27-story atrium was too large to renovate completely, so the design concentrated on the part guests see (close-up): the restaurant and lounge on the atrium floor level. Existing fabric canopies were removed to allow construction of elaborate gazebo-like wood structures which enclose the food and beverage areas. The wrought iron railings and cupolas give the new works a French Quarter trademark, while the simplified classical order of the columns blurs their traditional design enough so that they do not clash with relentless contemporary styling of the building.
Bottom photograph by Karl Francetic; photograph (right) by Ken Glaser.

NEW OLD LOOK

The renovation added traditional motifs, expensive materials and intricate detailing to the lobby to alleviate the free-form, omnivalent quality of its original design. French- and Spanish-inspired chairs, settees and tables are grouped around Tai Ping rugs in formal seating clusters to break up the space and order it in an understandable way. The renovation removed huge mobiles in the two-story spaces at each end of the lobby (top), replacing them with 12-foot high chandeliers (bottom). In the lower area in between, the original flat ceilings (center left) were modified with new vaults which feature wrought iron and crystal chandeliers (center right).

Top and center left photographs by Newmark Diercks; center right photograph by Ken Glaser; bottom photograph by Karl Francetic.

La Quinta Inns
Reimaging Program for all Properties in Chain

In most chains, headquarters keeps an eye on renovations, but is not responsible for the design concept and does not check the details to assure a uniform look. Not so at La Quinta Inns, where headquarters created a single renovation design and then executed it at more than 220 properties in less than a year. The unusual renovation process, tellingly named a "reimaging program," reflects the profile and business strategy of the budget motel chains - to produce a uniform look, and do it in a hurry.

LOBBY LOGO
The reimaging project added towers (facing page) to many properties and reworked those already in place. The chain's new logo (above) is a prominent feature on the towers, which serve to tell freeway drivers where and what La Quinta motels are. At properties where drivers would not be able to see a tower from the interstate, or where the building or sign were already very visible, no tower was added.
Photographs by La Quinta Inns, Inc.

Name	La Quinta Inns
Location	More than 220 motels in 29 states Headquarters: San Antonio, Texas
Owner	La Quinta Inns, Inc.
Operator	La Quinta Inns, Inc.
Type of Hotel	Economy-priced motel
Date of Original Construction	First motel: 1968
Number of Rooms	Approximately 26,000
Bars & Restaurants	None in typical property
Recreation Facilities	Outdoor pool in typical property
Type of Renovation	Properties open during renovation
Cost	$55 million
Date	May 1993 - June 1994
Architect and Interior Designer	Design Concept: Fugleberg Koch Architects, Winter Park, Florida
Consultants	Marketing and Design: SBG Partners, San Francisco, California Advertising Agency: GSD&M, Austin, Texas

GUIDING PRINCIPLE
To simplify the task of designing a renovation for more than 220 motels, the designers made a "kit of parts." The "kit" identified the redesigned elements, such as the landscaping, porte cochere repaving, the new tower, and exterior architectural trim and railings shown in this rendering of the master design concept (top).
Rendering by Fugleberg Koch Architects.

GREEN EVOLUTION
In a move to make the properties appear more welcoming and residential, and to differentiate them from institutional-looking competitors, the renovation team added trees, shrubs and other landscaping (bottom) to soften the main elevations of the buildings (left). The arches over the top-floor windows and at roof level in the center of the building were part of the "kit of parts." The arches also display prominently the new company logo.
Photographs by La Quinta Inns, Inc.

Redesigning franchise properties can be as easy as herding cats, but La Quinta had a formidable advantage in executing a total makeover: almost all properties are company-owned. The firm was determined to take advantage of that fact to produce a uniform product appealing to its existing customers and inviting to new guests, and to execute the transformation practically overnight to maximize its impact. The low-price, limited-service chain, also sought to differentiate itself from competitors and increase revenues.

A prime motivation for the reimaging was the considerable variation among individual properties in the chain, which made it impossible for designers to produce one set of working drawings suitable for all buildings. Instead, La Quinta began with the big picture, putting together a team consisting of management and outside firms for architecture and interior design, advertising and corporate image. The team first chose the overall goals for the reimaging

and then attacked the details to produce what Trish Rhem, director of interiors for Fugleberg Koch, called a "kit of parts." Those design elements were then used by the individual teams La Quinta later put together to renovate each property. Many "parts" from the "kit" were used on practically every motel in the chain, but any time a particular design element was not appropriate for a specific property, it was not used there.

RED CARPET ARRIVAL
In addition to new planting, the reimaging changed the landscape treatment of hard surfaces. Existing asphalt paving was removed at the porte cochere and replaced with patterned concrete reminiscent of stone paving. The color of the new paving complements the roofing, which did not change.
Photographs by La Quinta Inns, Inc.

Although the reimaging did not reposition the chain in the market, it did move in a different position on the map for the source of the exterior style of the motels. The original motels had a "Mexican primitive" style (La Quinta means "country house" in Spanish); and the reimaging moved north of the border, so to speak, settling upon the "Santa Fe look" of the Southwestern United States instead. The existing earth-tone paint on the masonry walls and long beam and rafter extension were deemed heavy and unappealing, so the building exteriors were repainted in white to give a bright, crisp feeling, with green trim and matching bronze-patina railings and medallions. The beam and rafter extensions were shortened, and new arches and other architectural detailing were added to give a sense of richness and a residential quality. The design also included extensive changes to landscaping to increase "curb appeal" and lure first-time guests. Landscaping and building detail were added mostly on the front of the motels; where other sides of the building also acted as the entry to properties, they also received the exterior upgrades.

Gary Mead, the president and chief executive officer who had recently taken over the firm, ordered photographs of the signs of all the properties in the chain — and discovered that they were different sizes, shapes, and colors. Even the words on the signs varied — but they were all dull. He decided to redo the signs, the company logo, and even the name. The company streamlined its name from La Quinta Motor Inns, dropping "Motor" as outdated. The designers made a logo for the new name, brightening it with a Southwestern-blue background and yellow and purple sunburst. The number and placement of signs installed at each property during the renovations depended on sight lines from nearby roads and freeways.

The blues and purples carry over from the sign to the building exterior and then into the interiors. The quarry tile floors, brown and orange plastic laminates, and dark brown-stained woodwork were targeted as dull, institutional and uninviting like the exteriors. The designers added lighter flooring and furniture and additional architectural details, such as columns, faux stone and wall fountains to create warm, inviting, bright interiors. The renovations expanded each lobby to accommodate a new buffet for the free continental breakfast the chain had introduced just before reimaging began.

La Quinta launched a retraining program for employees to go along with the reimaging, augmented by new uniforms, a new advertising campaign, and a new slogan, "You're not staying at a hotel. You're staying with us."

When the reimaging program was complete, a guest survey showed that not only the exteriors and the lobbies, but also the guest rooms were rated higher than they had been before the makeover. That was quite a compliment, since the project did not include any changes to the guest rooms. This vote of confidence was not mistaken, just premature. La Quinta began planning and designing a program to upgrade the guest rooms late in 1994.

NEW COLORS, NEW SPACES
Lobbies received the most extensive redesign of any portion of the properties (opposite page, bottom). Existing fluorescent lighting was removed and replaced with incandescent fixtures, existing soffits were removed to make the lobbies feel more spacious, new registrations desks with lower counter heights were installed to make guests feel less separated from hotel staff, and new architectural columns helped define circulation areas and added detail (opposite page, right). While the existing lobbies feature a lot of dark browns (opposite page, left), the new palette consists of pale background colors with accents of greens, blues and orange. Those colors carry over from the new exterior treatment, as do the plants added in the reimaging. Faux-stone accents added to make lobbies more ornate and appealing include stone wall fountains (left).
Photographs by la Quinta Inns, Inc.

The Ritz-Carlton Kansas City
Kansas City, Missouri

Would you expect to find an understated Boston-Brahman hotel interior in a Moorish-theme shopping center in the middle of the Great Plains? If the property had the Ritz-Carlton name, you probably would, and if you checked into the Ritz-Carlton Kansas City in the Country Club Plaza shopping complex that's exactly what you would find. This combination is what was in store when the Ritz-Carlton Hotel Company teamed up with shopping center developer and previous hotel owner J.C. Nichols Company to transform the existing Alameda Plaza Hotel into a Ritz-Carlton.

Name	The Ritz-Carlton Kansas City
Location	Kansas City, Missouri
Owner	Ritz-Carlton Hotel Company
Operator	Ritz-Carlton Hotel Company
Type of Hotel	Luxury
Date of Original Construction	1972
Number of Rooms	374, including 28 suites and 15 with handicapped accessibility
Bars & Restaurants	4
Meeting Rooms Number & Size	11, plus 6 conference suites / 22,500 square feet
Recreation Facilities	Outdoor pool, fitness center with exercise equipment and aerobics area, sauna and steam room for men and women
Type of Renovation	All finishes, limited layout changes. Hotel open throughout renovation.
Cost	$30 million - $40 million
Date	May 1898 - February 1990
Architect	Milton Pate Associates, Atlanta, Georgia Linscott, Haylett, Wimmer & Wheat, Kansas City, Missouri
Interior Designer	Hirsch/Bedner & Associates, Atlanta, Georgia
Consultants	Sasaki Associates, San Francisco, California (landscape architects)
Contractor	J. E. Dunn

AGES APART
The airy, Mediterranean-contemporary informality of the Alameda Plaza lobby with rugged clay flooring and romantic furniture and accessories (facing page) gave way to the much more formal and precise mood of the paneled Ritz-Carlton lobby with its emphasis on 19th century-style English furniture (below).

The hotel, a curved twelve-story tower with a six-story wing housing public spaces, had opened as a luxury property in 1972 to broaden the scope of the upscale shopping center. By the late 1980s, the hotel was poised for a larger role, and the renovation had to transform it into part of the Ritz-Carlton chain — without requiring a shutdown. With neighbors like Gucci and Saks Fifth Avenue in the 55-acre shopping complex, there was no problem with the location. There was only one obstacle separating the existing hotel from its new siblings in the Ritz-Carlton chain: image. The existing hotel extended the Moorish look to the interior, but when Ritz-Carlton became the innkeeper, it was time for Ali Baba to check out.

While the Moorish theme survives on the exterior to make the hotel compatible with the surrounding retail complex, the interior has become by-the-book Ritz-Carlton. The chain's hotels are not clones, but the common palette of rich wood casework and paneling, tapestries, draperies, and oil paintings is the basis for the interior of each property to remind guests of the ambiance of the original Ritz-Carlton in Boston or the grand antecedent, the Ritz in Paris.

The designers left intact the floor-to-ceiling windows typical of post World War II construction, and more appropriate for the airy feeling of the Kansas City location than smaller, but more traditional glazing might have been. They removed the Moorish arches and ceilings, clay-tile floors, plaster walls and rough-timber detailing that had been used to make the Alameda Plaza complement the retail complex outside, and built an interior enclave of wood paneling, restrained carpeting, 18th and 19th century art and antiques in public spaces, and Drexel Heritage reproduction furniture in guest rooms.

AIRY TO ELEGANT
The former Pam Pam West was a diner which served up informal food from an open kitchen at counters and banquettes. The spaces, lighting, styles and materials were loosely modeled on the building's overall theme to complement lighter dining (left). When Ritz-Carlton designers remade the space, the kitchen was relegated to back-of-the-house and the eatery was redefined with more formal spaces, sconces and chandeliers, reproduction antique furniture and detailed wall moldings (below). The Cafe continues to serve simpler fare; light colors, open spaces and lack of wood wall paneling distinguish it from the fine dining Rooftop Restaurant.

NIGHT MOVES, RIGHT MOVES
The former Rooftop Lounge struck a tone of Old World intrigue, with fanciful arches and low lighting (left). Remodeled as The Bar, the space looks like the haunts of England's old boy network, with hunting prints, reproduction side tables, a fireplace and full-paneled walls (below).

The guest rooms and public spaces required relatively few changes in layout, and the back-of-the-house needed no significant reconfiguration. The biggest change in layout was the expansion of the two-story main ballroom by eliminating a meeting room which had intruded into its upper-level. New movable partitions allow the 12,000 square foot ballroom to be divided into four smaller spaces. The change added eleven percent to the meeting space available in the building. Creation of the chain's signature Ritz-Carlton Club on the top two guest room floors required adding a private connecting stair and eliminating three guest rooms to make space for the club lounge. Two or three existing rooms were combined to create each new suite in the renovated building.

Guest rooms were completely renovated with individual refrigerators with honor bars, safes, computer modem connections, and Italian marble bathrooms with telephones and hair dryers. The new business center offers amenities including fax, teleconferencing, copying, and secretarial service.

The existing outdoor pool was augmented with a new indoor fitness center with exercise equipment, an aerobics area, and sauna and steam room for men and women. Existing poolside landscaping at the Garden Terrace was refined and trees, shrubs, and flowers were added at the motor entrance to establish the property's new character before guests see the interior.

GREENER PASTURES Although the striking and unmistakable exterior of the structure retained its original appearance during the remodeling (below), landscaping was added at the motor entrance to the site of more than three acres to make the property more appealing from the point where guests first see it (left).

ROOFTOP FACELIFT

Diners at the property's top eatery look out over Kansas City, but the interior before the renovation might have suggested Marrakech or Damascus with its white and brown color theme, Mediterranean materials and Thousand-and-One-Nights ceiling (right). The renovated Rooftop Restaurant strikes a simpler tone with rich carpeting throughout, extensive wall paneling, and art and armchairs which suggest an understated club atmosphere (below).

FROM HAREM TO HARROD'S
The Mediterranean theme continued into the guest rooms before the renovation, with bright white walls, dark-wood-and-wrought-iron accessories and ornately carved headboards (left). Renovated rooms have muted wall colors and furniture intended to evoke London, not the Near East (below).

PUSHING THE ENVELOPE
The renovation extended the original ballroom and eliminated a meeting room which had intruded on the upper level of the two-story space, creating a low-ceilinged zone at one end of the room. The new ballroom has a uniform two-story ceiling throughout; the space can be subdivided into four "Salons" with sound-insulated moveable partitions.

The Houstonian Hotel

Houston, Texas

Never a run-of-the-mill operation, the Houstonian Campus chalked up quite a few distinctions by the time Redstone Properties acquired it in 1992. Its latest distinction - bankruptcy attracted the turnaround management firm and engendered a makeover to redefine and redirect the unusual but unsuccessful property.

RANCH WITH A PEDIGREE
The new lobby of the hotel illustrates the market strategy of the renovation. The Houstonian derived significant room sales from meetings in the 1980s, and when meetings slackened, the hotel operation went into the red. The renovation disengaged the two market segments, aiming at filling guest rooms with upscale frequent individual travelers. A large restaurant which had catered to meetings before the renovation was removed and replaced with this "great room" which recalls an urbane but earthy Texas hunting lodge or ranch.
Photograph by Richard Payne.

Name	The Houstonian Hotel
Location	Houston, Texas
Owner	Redstone Hotels, Inc., Houston, Texas
Operator	Redstone Hotels, Inc.
Type of Hotel	Luxury
Date of Original Construction	1980
Number of Rooms	292
Bars & Restaurants	4; one in hotel, three in other buildings in complex
Meeting Rooms Number & Size	34 rooms / 33,000 square feet
Recreation Facilities	Private fitness club with 25-meter pool, gymnasium, jogging track, exercise equipment, racquetball, handball, squash and tennis courts, rock-climbing wall. Separate spa with exercise, beauty and weight-loss facilities.
Type of Renovation	Phased renovation; hotel open throughout renovation
Cost	Hotel: $14 million; Fitness Club: $2.5 million
Date	June 1993 - April 1994
Architect	Public Spaces: Good Fulton & Farrell, Dallas
Interior Designer	Guest Rooms: Daiker Howard, Dallas; Fitness Club: HOK Houston Manor House and Public Spaces: Vivian/Nichols Associates Inc., Dallas
Consultants	Mechanical, Electrical and Plumbing Engineers: B. L. & P. Engineers, Dallas; Structural Engineers: The Sadler Group, Fort Worth
Contractor	Guest Rooms and Public Spaces: Case & Associates, Houston; Fitness Club, Roofing: Constructors & Associates, Houston

The Houstonian was constructed as a multifaceted campus at the end of the 1970s, with the Houstonian Hotel, a medical fitness center, a conference center, and an office building on its 18 acres, previously occupied by several large houses. Each piece was supposed to fit with the others, making a profitable network. Things didn't work out that way, and even though it boasted the President as a legal resident, the operation foundered.

When the new owner Redstone began the renovation in early 1993, it set out to reinforce the athletic club, the conference facility and a separate women's health spa in the complex to capitalize on their strength. Redstone calculated that the hotel's 300 rooms constituted just ten percent of the overall hotel capacity in the retail hub around the nearby Galleria mall. By upgrading, the new owners aimed to attract the frequent individual travelers at the top of that market to make the hotel operation profitable, too.

The hotel-conference center, fitness club, and health spa are in separate buildings, so Redstone selected individual designers for each one, providing an overall design statement and coordinating their work. The project began with the guest rooms, then the fitness club, then the spa, the conference center and finally, the public spaces of the hotel.

KITCHEN VIFW
The Cafe provides diners with a novel view of the kitchen, without the bother of noises, smells or even a window to wash. The trompe-l'oeil mural of a European kitchen scene, executed by a Dallas artist, also complements the color scheme of the restaurant. Imposing banquettes are balanced by country farm and wicker chairs.
Photograph by Richard Payne.

INFORMAL PRESTIGE
The Bar, a stylized interpretation of the Ruhlmann period, balances an affluent atmosphere with more informal touches. Chessboard tabletops suggest a brainy, leisurely crowd, while the nude painting reminds us that this is a men's bar in Texas. Hardwood floors, burled wainscoting and silk upholstery are tip-offs that it is oil men, not cowboys, who come here for drinks.
Photograph by Richard Payne.

CLASSIC MEETS CONTEMPORARY
The Presidential Suite mixes traditional and current design themes. Armchairs are a modified contemporary version of the Martha Washington chair, with bold red cotton moirè fabric. The sleek glass top of the table reveals traditional console supports, while timeless elements such as the chandelier and the antique reproduction sideboard balance the modern windows.
Photograph by Richard Payne.

Completed in 1980, the four-story main hotel building is most notable as the legal residence George Bush maintained in Houston during his employment at a more famous address in Washington, D.C. The unobtrusive modern exterior did not change in the renovation because Redstone wanted to emphasize the lush existing landscaping on the campus, not the buildings. The renovated public rooms are designed to look like an elegant but informal country lodge of a Texas millionaire, set fortuitously ten minutes from the center of Houston. The original generic contemporary lobby and registration areas were gutted and reconfigured so that guests enter the registration area and proceed to the main lobby, which is modeled after the "great room" of a wilderness lodge. Wood flooring with area rugs, plush sofas, and iron light fixtures help create the lodge atmosphere, focusing on a two-sided fireplace of Texas proportions. A monumental metal stair to the mezzanine level was added in the registration area.

Guest rooms received new custom-patterned drapes and bedspreads and traditional Kimball armoires, desks, and tables. Bathrooms were redone with marble floors and vanities. Each room has a two-line speaker phone with data port, a telephone in the bathroom, a mini bar, and a choice of 35 movies on the television in addition to the usual cable fare. Guest rooms retain their original layout, except that seven new suites were created by combining individual rooms. All the existing suites, except the one occupied by the Bushes, were divided back into separate rooms. The top floor was upgraded as a new concierge level with a 2,000 square foot concierge lounge and a business center. Its guest rooms have upgraded finishes and higher ceilings.

QUIET LUXURY
Guest rooms have traditional furniture; custom fabrics; soft, simple colors; and understated moldings.
The simple window treatment takes advantage of the floor-to-ceiling windows of the contemporary
building, providing a close-up view of the thick canopy of trees outdoors.
Photograph by Richard Payne.

FAME, FORTUNE AND FITNESS
The 125,000 square foot Fitness Center at the Houstonian isn't your average gym, and with initiation fees that run into the four figures, it attracts Houston's movers and shakers, not the average Joe. The renovation started with such workaday elements as a new roof, and then got into the serious work of making the center reflect the lifestyle — both economic and athletic — of the members. Before the renovation, the exercise room was a sea of weights and machines, with a warehouse atmosphere created partly by its unfinished ceiling (below). To make the workout flow clear and effective, the renovation (left and opposite page bottom) divided the space into separate zones for cardiovascular, free weight and stretching and toning work, using different flooring and ceiling materials instead of building walls to separate the zones and define circulation areas (hatched paths in drawing at top of opposite page). The ceilings were painted a tough-looking black and light fixtures were relocated to relate to the design below them. Users enter the workout area at the cardiovascular area (photograph at intersection of path in; right hand side of drawing), where the energy level is high, and can go to the stretching and toning area (top of drawing) when they want to cool down away from the stimulus of others' workouts. Next to the cardiovascular area (center of right hand zone of the drawing), exercise machines and the free weight area flank the circulation path, and at the bottom is a boxing ring (foreground in bottom photograph, opposite page; bottom zone oriented on the diagonal in the drawing). The windows at the perimeter of the workout room were left unobstructed to give members a good view of the greenery outside the building. The renovation also redid the locker rooms (top and bottom rooms immediately to the left of the workout room in the drawing).
Photographs and drawing provided courtesy of HOK Houston.

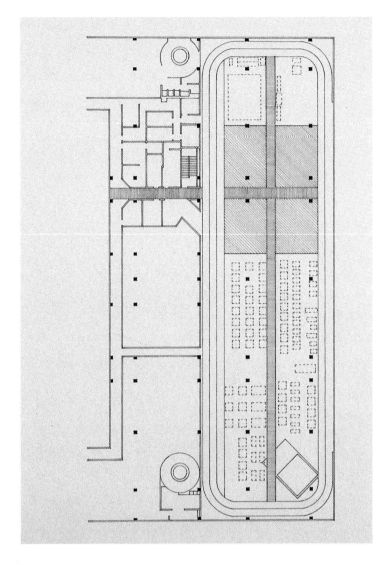

Over the years, the original medical fitness center evolved into a high-end recreation business and the most profitable part of the Houstonian Campus, with initiation fees of $4,500 to $12,500 and 3,200 names on its membership roster. The 125,000 square foot club, also available to hotel guests, has a 25-meter pool, a full-court gymnasium, a banked indoor running track with pacing lights, an exercise room, racquetball, handball, squash and tennis courts, a rock-climbing wall, men's and women's sauna and massage rooms, and facilities for medical evaluations. A $2.5 million updating gave the athletic facility new locker rooms, new exercise equipment and conversion of one racquetball court into a computer-simulation golf clinic.

The separate Phoenix Spa is located in a 1930s mansion which is now part of the campus. It offers a beauty and health regimen for women who want to lose weight, exercise or get treatments. Clients can come for day use or stay in one of the five guest rooms in the self-contained facility, which also has its own dining room and special menu. The 1994 renovation of the spa gave it new finishes throughout, with no major changes of fixtures, equipment or room layout. The Manor House restaurant occupies a Georgian-style house built on the campus before the hotel. It received new fixtures and finishes and a marble bar.

The renovation of the conference center building and hotel meeting rooms includes new leather armchairs for 20 in the executive boardroom, which has a private patio and balcony. No changes in room layouts were made, but new audio-visual systems were installed.

Sheraton Harbor Island Hotel
San Diego, California

Running hard to stay ahead of a hot nearby rival is a predicament familiar to many hotel owners and operators; ITT Sheraton and Harbor Cal San Diego found themselves in an odd twist on this familiar tale: they owned the hotel which was giving them unwelcome competition. To remedy the problem, they folded the Sheraton Grand on Harbor Isla d into the larger Sheraton Harbor Island operation just three hundred yards away, and did so with a fast-tracked design-build renovation that reads like the hotel version of Japanese "just in time" manufacturing techniques.

Name	**Sheraton Harbor Island Hotel**
Location	**San Diego, California**
Owner	**Harbor Cal San Diego**
Operator	**ITT Sheraton Corporation**
Type of Hotel	**Convention / Resort**
Date of Original Construction	**East tower: 1972; west tower: 1969**
Number of Rooms	**1,048**
Bars & Restaurants	**Harbor's Edge, Waterworks, Bakery, Quinn's Bar, Lobby Lounge**
Meeting Rooms (Number & Size)	**42 / 73,000 square feet**
Recreation Facilities	**Sand volleyball courts, marina with sailboats and jet ski rentals, two pools, tennis, children'srecreation center, spa and fitness center with exercise and weight equipment, body andbeauty treatments**
Type of Renovation	**Phased renovation, no total shutdown**
Cost	**$32 million**
Date	**1994 - 1995**
Architect	**Wimberly Allison Tong & Goo, Newport Beach, California**
Interior Designer	**Wilson & Associates**
Consultants	**Food Service: Thomas Ricca Associates, Engelwood, Colorado**
	Lighting: Bouyea & Associates, Dallas, Texas
	Landscape Design: Peridian Inc., Irvine, California
Contractor	**Charles Pankow Builders, Ltd.**

FLORAL EFFUSION
Landscaping changes included additional palm trees and grass, plus a variety of flower areas and ornamental plants and grasses (above). A number of new fountains enliven the landscape, each with a specific character tailored to its location. At the stair to the east tower swimming pool area, a whale sculpture on axis with the main building entrance reinforces the ocean theme of the marina setting. The one-story restaurant in the background was extended during the renovation; before the remodeling, a smaller restaurant overlooked a recreation area of hard surfaces and sand (facing page).

The $32 million project required only six months for design work and four months for the major portion of construction, with phases overlapped constantly. Followed up by another four-month construction phase for the second half of the property a year later, the renovation corrected a mixed metaphor of marketing which had been an impediment ever since 1979, when Sheraton took over what were originally designed as two separate hotels at San Diego's Harbor Island marina. The smaller Sheraton Grand boasted large upscale rooms, but guests were not always keen to pay higher rates than those charged by the larger Sheraton Harbor Island only a stone's throw away. The solution was to combine the two, repositioning them at the upper end of the convention market which provides about 70 percent of their market.

The project began with the commission to the Newport Beach, California, office of architects Wimberly Allison Tong & Goo. WATG prepared a design concept in two months for the repositioning of the larger east tower (formerly the Harbor Island), including a gut of the public spaces, new pools and landscaping, new food and beverage outlets, additional meeting rooms, and a make-over of the health club. Then contractor Charles Pankow came on board, putting pricing packages together as WATG spent the next four months on the construction documents. Before the documents were complete, the project went in for a building permit and the approval of the San Diego Port Authority, which owns the site. Construction was under way by the time the finishing touches had been made on the design. The east tower reopened in the spring of 1994.

Changes at the east tower are apparent to guests before they reach the building. New landscaping and a new porte cochere introduce a realigned entry and a new lobby with a view of the marina, something guests did not get before the renovation. The four food and beverage outlets in the east tower before the renovation were replaced by three, dominated by a new three-meal restaurant with massive windows overlooking the marina.

BILLOWING SAILS
The new Waterworks poolside bar and restaurant took a novel approach to the nautical theme in replacing an existing stucco-and-tile-roof food and beverage outlet. Its wave-form roof is framed with round pipe stock and covered in canvas to make a visual link with the sailboats tied up in the slips at the marina.

MAKING A GRAND ENTRANCE
The new east tower lobby continues the exotic resort theme of the exterior landscaping. A trellis-like wood grid spans the room, revealing a ceiling painted with a trompe-l'oeil sky. The lobby offers clear sight lines through the hotel and out to the marina; arriving guests had to negotiate a series of turns to catch a glimpse of the marina before the renovation.

NEW APPROACH
Before the renovation, guests arriving at the main east tower got out of their cars under a long, narrow canopy and passed through doors which led directly to the elevator core (above, left). The arrangement was direct and efficient for those already familiar with the hotel, but the renovation designers decided to provide a more formal and welcoming arrival sequence for the benefit of newcomers. A large porte cochere makes the arrival point look more substantial, and the entry doors lead to the new lobby which overlooks the marina (above, right).

Renovated accessible guest rooms brought the property into compliance with the Americans with Disabilities Act. On the exterior, L-shaped swimming pools gave way to serpentine ones with seahorse sculptures at their perimeter. The renovation increased the number and variety of landscaping features, stressing free and curvilinear forms to foster a resort image. The health club was gutted and redesigned, with treatment rooms added to its exercise and relaxation facilities. A year after construction shut down the east tower for its four-month metamorphosis, construction crews arrived at the west tower (formerly the Sheraton Grand on Harbor Island) for a similar period, rebuilding the lobby and meeting spaces, putting new finishes in the restaurant, renovating all 350 guest rooms and updating the heating and air-conditioning system. Because the towers are separate and only one was closed at a time, the renovation never required a complete shutdown of the property. But because Sheraton already had advance bookings for meetings by the time the renovation project received the corporate go-ahead, even a partial shutdown meant farming out solid business to other properties.

To limit the loss - and to avoid turning away future bookings - the owner and operator fast-tracked design and construction. Southern California's economic downturn worked to their advantage, providing an ample supply of construction contractors willing to complete the job in short order. The fast-paced strategy proved that "If you can't beat 'em, join 'em" even applies when two competitors have the same parent.

RESORT AMBIANCE
The renovation replaced two L-shaped swimming pools with new free-form ones which complement the organic curvilinear forms of the new landscaping elements. The seahorse sculpture is a fountain which shoots water into the pool.

LIGHTEN UP
The exterior massing of the buildings did not change overall, but the renovation sought to give them a softer, lighter quality by repainting in a peach tone and replacing some of the rectilinear shapes on the roof line with arcs (below). The new curved hood at the top of the elevator tower also provided a spot for the Sheraton crest, something lacking on the marina side of the building before the renovation (right).

Hotel Macdonald
Edmonton, Alberta

How many times has a renovation team been commissioned to restore the grandeur of a historic property, with the Catch-22 that most of the property is a bland recent expansion, an eyesore but a necessity on the balance sheet? And how often do the designers wish they could just tear down the addition and give the owners and operators what they literally asked for: the famous hotel, restored to its historic grandeur. It took eight years, two owners, and a fluctuating local economy, but when the renovation of the Hotel Macdonald in Edmonton was complete, the final outcome matched the first impulse of the team.

TOWN AND COUNTRY
While the office buildings of Edmonton practically come to its front door step, the Macdonald has plenty of breathing room on the other side, where the green valley of the North Saskatchewan River opens a wide vista.
Photograph by Mary Nichols.

Name	Hotel Macdonald
Location	Edmonton, Alberta
Owner	Canadian Pacific Hotels and Resorts
Operator	Canadian Pacific Hotels and Resorts
Type of Hotel	Luxury
Date of Original Construction	1915
Number of Rooms	198
Bars & Restaurants	Harvest Room / Library Bar
Meeting Rooms Number & Size	8 / 13,400 square feet
Recreation Facilities	Health club, including indoor pool, sauna, steam room, squash, exercise machines, game room
Type of Renovation	Hotel closed during construction; guest-room floors reconfigured
Cost	$28 million (Canadian)
Date	1988 - 1991
Architect	IBI Group, Edmonton, Alberta
Interior Designer	Heather Jones & Associates, Toronto, Ontario
Consultants	Structural Engineer: Read Jones Christoffersen Mechanical Engineer: Hemisphere Engineering, Inc.
Contractor	Stuart Olson Construction

ENTER A DIFFERENT AGE

As soon as guests reach the lobby, they can see that historic inspiration was not just an exterior treatment that stopped at the front door. The renovation extended the original wall paneling in the lobby (below) higher to give the room a more calm and serene quality. The oak pilasters and entablature were added to make the arched opening to the Confederation Lounge more formal and visually articulate. The adjacent registration area (left) features faux-finish plaster detailing around wall openings which imitates the limestone on the exterior of the building. It did not exist in the lobby before the renovation, but appears in a historic ballroom photograph.

Photograph by Mary Nichols

Completed by the Grand Trunk Railway in 1915, the Hotel Macdonald put Edmonton on the map of the golden age of Canadian railroad hotel building. Reminiscent of a Renaissance chateau, with an Indiana limestone exterior and large, formal public rooms with Edwardian interiors, it was one of a group of properties the railroads constructed to fill passenger trains by luring affluent guests to cross Canada. Forty years later, as elite travelers with steamer trunks and nannies disappeared from sleeping cars and mass middle-class travel took over, the owners remade the Macdonald to fit the current hotel profile. They added a modern 15-story tower, dwarfing the original building, which they transformed on the interior. The up-to-date design did not succeed in the long run, and the property closed in 1983 after a gradual decline.

Then-owner Canadian National Hotels studied what to do with the property, and in 1985, the City of Edmonton designated the building and its Confederation Lounge, lobby, Wedgwood Room and Empire Ballroom as a Municipal Heritage Resource, putting on the pressure to preserve it. CN joined with a local real estate company on an ambitious renovation, demolishing the addition in 1986, but it floundered in a slow economy. CN sold its hotel chain to rival Canadian Pacific Hotels in 1988, and the renovation got back on track the following year. The final outcome returned the hotel, which is perched on a bluff at the edge of downtown Edmonton overlooking the North Saskatchewan River, to the prominent place in the hospitality market it had occupied when it opened.

Demolition of the tower addition on the city side of the hotel made room for a new formal garden which acts as an urban forecourt and shows off the traditional exterior amidst Edmonton's modern high-rise buildings. On the river side, the renovation added gardens and exposed the basement floor where new meeting space and a health club were added. On the interior, the most important public spaces were restored to their original design. Major ground-floor rooms such as the Confederation Lounge, the Empire Ballroom, and the Wedgwood Room were restored to their historic appearance. Other rooms were modified or redesigned in a manner compatible with the original building; rooms on the mezzanine overlooking the lobby were reworked as meeting rooms.

Although the renovation demolished the tower and barely added any space to the original building, it actually increased guest room space by two floors. The area under the steeply sloping roof which had previously been used for staff bedrooms, storage, a printing shop and air-handling equipment became new suites, four of them two stories high. Windows which follow the roof plane provide light to the new rooms without requiring construction of dormers. The existing guest room floors needed a complete reworking — some guest rooms had no bathrooms before the renovation. The renovation added bathrooms, increased the size of guest rooms and the room count in the original building from 196 to 198.

HISTORIC PATTERN
The Wedgwood Room, named after the fine china because of its intricate detailing, is located in the octagonal tower at one end of the building. Over the years, it was home to the Edmonton Press Club - and to visiting U.S. soldiers during World War II. The plaster fresco on the domed ceiling was restored by hand during the renovation.
Photograph by Mary Nichols.

ROOTS OF THE NATION
In the Confederation Lounge, the restoration work included an embossed ceiling with ornamental plasterwork designed by Canadian artist Arthur Hasley and a 9-by-18 foot Frederick Challener painting of the Fathers of Confederation, copied after an original which was lost in a fire in Ottawa. One of three rooms where historical accuracy was tantamount, it was almost indistinguishable after the renovation (below) from its condition in a historic photograph (right). The window treatment of whimsical heavy lace and brocades is new; it was chosen to allow a lot of light in and leaven the sober atmosphere of the room.
Historic photograph provided courtesy of the Alberta Provincial Museum Archive.
Renovation photograph by Mary Nichols.

IT DISAPPEARED OVERNIGHT
The addition constructed in the 1950s
towered over the hotel, bearing its name
like a sign of the times to the public
(above). Time was unkind to the addition,
which is nowhere to be seen in a similar
view taken after the renovation (right).
Photograph by Mary Nichols.

SERVICE AND AMBIANCE
The Harvest Room restaurant
occupies a desirable ground
floor location with a view of
the private hotel gardens and
the river valley below. The only
thing not close at hand before
the renovation was the kitchen,
but that problem was solved
by moving the kitchen to a
main floor space next to the
restaurant.
Photograph by Mary Nichols.

TALKING, DRINKING AND EATING ALLOWED
The Library Bar has bookshelves, wood paneling, and a refined atmosphere, but
guests don't need to fear angering the librarian if
they want to have a cocktail and a conversation.
Photograph by Mary Nichols.

GREENER PASTURES
Landscaping at the back of the hotel created a series of private gardens overlooking the North Saskatchewan River (left) which are heavily used for events during the summer. Focal points include a new gazebo (bottom, left) and fountain (bottom, right).
Photograph by Mary Nichols.

The renovation included the new mechanical and electrical systems, accessibility improvements, fire alarm and fire sprinklers usually associated with a major building overhaul, and a few less common infrastructure upgrades, including new exit stairs and vertical and horizontal fire separations. The elevators, which had been removed when the addition was constructed, were rebuilt in their original location, with new penthouses to allow them to reach the new suites in the former attic.

Exterior work was fitted closely to the interior renovations on both sides of the building. A new ballroom gallery and pre-function room were tied to the new park in front of the building where the tower addition previously stood.

All these changes add up to a bold restoration of the building, offering guests a chance to experience a hotel from another age without having to give up modern amenities. But why would an owner give up the tower addition, with more than 250 guest rooms and additional meeting rooms?

The answer: for a major market reposition. When it closed in 1983, the Macdonald had sunk to lower regions of the hotel market, but when it returned, it was the most prestigious - and most expensive - hotel in town. At the Macdonald, the literal interpretation of restoring a grand historic hotel started with the building and carried through to the product, as well.

WATER IN THE BASEMENT
Many renovations try to keep it out, but at the Macdonald a major accomplishment was adding a swimming pool and spa to the basement as part of the new health club.
Photograph by Mary Nichols.

RESTORED TO THE THRONE

The Empire Ballroom (above) remained relatively unchanged through the early 1950s (below), but later its original design was usurped when a rathskeller-style interior with a low ceiling was inserted in the space. During the renovation the half-timber ceiling of the impostor was removed, exposing the original one, which was restored and painted to match its original design (top, opposite page). The renovation augmented the ballroom with a new pre-function room and gallery (left) connecting to the rest of the hotel. Its construction enabled the renovation team to convert the existing corridor to the ballroom into kitchen space, thus improving service access to food and beverage operations.
Renovation photograph by Mary Nichols.

LADIES AND GENTLEMEN
The Jasper Room, a meeting room on the mezzanine level, is located in the former Gentlemen's Writing Room, which was set aside for men in the original hotel. The nearby Ladies' Drawing Room was provided for women to await their male escorts before entering lobby, which they were not permitted to do alone. The Drawing Room has become a meeting space, and yes, ladies are now permitted to appear unescorted in the lobby.
Photograph by Mary Nichols.

THE DETAILS OF HISTORY
The original door hardware displays the initials of the Grand Trunk Railway, the line which built the hotel. The renovation refinished and retained the hardware.
Photograph by Mary Nichols.

LIGHT, BRIGHT, AND RELAXING
Guest rooms and suites have a residential quality, with light color schemes; prints
of fishing flies and equestrian scenes reflect themes from the area. Furniture
influences are mostly turn-of-the-century.
Photograph by Mary Nichols.

ON THE STREETS OF TIME
A historic view of the end of the building from
100th Street shows the hotel almost identical to
its condition after the renovation.
Photograph provided courtesy of the
Alberta Provincial Museum Archive.

NOT A HUMBLE GARRET

The renovation created eight new suites in former attic space on the eighth and ninth floors, but they are unlikely to be occupied by bohemians traveling on a limited budget. Four of the suites cover two stories, with private stairs connecting the living and sleeping areas. The sloped walls and complex geometry created by the roof are used to enliven the space or accent important elements such as the soaking tub in the bathroom (center). The 2,500 square foot, two-floor Royal Suite (top) has two bedrooms, three baths, and a living room large enough to entertain 50 people. Oversize furniture matches the scale of its living room; the seating can be moved from the center of the room to the walls for large receptions. A large single guest room on the suite floor (bottom) has a seating area, beds with fancy duvets and a warm color scheme to combat the effect of short days during Edmonton's long winters.

Photograph by Mary Nichols.

The Chateau Frontenac
Quebec City, Quebec

The Chateau Frontenac might strike guests as a rambling, artful monument symbolizing everything that characterizes the city of Quebec which surrounds it. Those who notice that the property has been remodeled and expanded would discover that the recent project likewise seems to encompass all the elements of hotel renovation from A to Z. The phased updating includes reworking public spaces, adding new facilities to keep up with changes in the hospitality industry, replacing worn finishes and fixtures, conserving the cherished historical image of the property and, at the same time, carefully crafting new imagery.

FITNESS AND FUNCTION
At the tip of the roof above the fitness center in the addition is a large cooling tower exhaust grille, detailed to match the seams in the copper roofing around it. The architects placed a light inside the grille to illuminate the escaping vapor stream at night, adding a high-tech modern wrinkle to the imposing castle-like form of the building.
Photograph by Denis Farley.

Name	*The Chateau Frontenac*
Location	*Quebec City, Quebec*
Owner	*CP Hotels and Resorts*
Operator	*CP Hotels and Resorts*
Type of Hotel	*Luxury*
Date of Original Construction	*1893*
Number of Rooms	*610*
Bars & Restaurants	*Le Champlain, Caf de la Terrasse, Bar Saint-Laurent, Vranda Saint-Laurent, Bistro*
Meeting Rooms (Number & Size)	*20 / 22,000 square feet*
Recreation Facilities	*Indoor swimming pool; fitness center*
Type of Renovation	*Phased renovation and addition; hotel open throughout*
Cost	*$57,000,000 (Canadian)*
Date of Renovation	*1987 - 1993*
Architects	*Renovation of existing hotel: Dorval & Fortin and St. Gelais, Tremblay & Belanger, Quebec Design of new wing: Le Groupe Arcop, Montreal*
Interior Designer	*Alexandra Champalimaud et Assocís, Montreal*
Consultants	*Mechanical, Electrical & Structural Engineers: Solivar Groupe-Conseil, Quebec Mechanical and Electrical Engineers: Liboiron Roy Caron et Assocís, Montreal Landscape Architect: Sandra Donaldson, Montreal*
Contractor	*Renovations: Beauvais et Varret Inc., Les Constructions Bland et Lapointe Inc., Construction B S L Inc., Beauvais & Marquis Inc., J.E. Verreault & Fils Lte, Quebec New Wing: J. E. Verreault et Fils Lte, Quebec*

SETTING THE CITYSCAPE
Set on the Cape Diamond promontory overlooking the Quebec City, the
Chateau Frontenac gives visitors the feeling of staying in a European castle as
they look out over the rooftops below.

The fortress-like hotel, built by the Canadian Pacific Railroad in 1893, underwent its last major renovation in 1973, when CP embarked on a program to counter the "stuffy" image for which some critics had reproached the property. That project retained the overall image and most of the details of the historic building, while inserting some more "up-to-date" features and designs. As the 100th birthday of the property approached, CP Hotels and Resorts launched a multi-faceted project, this time stressing faithfulness to history in the existing portion of the building and steering design innovations into an addition and back-of-the-house facilities.

The hotel was built by William Van Horne, president of Canadian Pacific, with the design by influential U.S. architect Bruce Price. The original building, called the Riverview Wing, had 170 rooms and three suites. Its success led to construction of the Citadel Wing in 1899, followed by the Mont-Carmel Wing in 1908, and later the Saint Louis Wing and finally the Central Tower.

In 1987 and 1988, guest rooms in the Mont Carmel and Riverview wings and the lower floors of the Central Tower were renovated. From 1989 to 1993, the guest rooms in the St. Louis Wing and on the upper floors of the Central Tower underwent renovation, along with food and beverage outlets, the retail spaces and the exterior area at the entry. The alterations converted some storage and staff sleeping rooms on the top floor into additional guest rooms, while combining small existing guest rooms to create one or two larger rooms out of two or three existing rooms. In addition to finishes and furniture-fixtures-and-equipment overhaul, the renovation included life safety and building systems upgrades and rationalization of back-of-the-house areas, including a reconfiguration which made the main kitchen more compact to allow better access and circulation for meeting rooms.

When the CP and its architects began designing a new health club for the hotel, they knew they would have to deal very carefully with the strict historic preservation review by the city of Quebec, but they were in for a surprise: city officials urged them to make the addition larger than they had originally planned. The renovation team willingly followed the city's suggestion, erecting the new Claude Pratte Wing over the existing parking garage which adjoined the hotel.

As a result, the four-story wing, completed in 1993, has not only a fitness center and outdoor terrace, but 66 new guest rooms.

The addition posed a number of challenges, but the renovation team saw them as opportunities to weave the new construction into the warp and woof of the historic building. Guest-room configurations had to change from floor to floor where floor plates shrink under the steep roof which takes up half the height of the

addition. Although the exterior materials of the addition are almost identical to those of the existing hotel, their brand new appearance contrasts with the weathered look of the historic building. The difference is easy to see today, but in 50 years it won't be, said architect Bruce Allen of Le Groupe Arcop. That might seem like a long time, but in the perspective of the Chateau Frontenac, it is just another link in a very long chain.

THE SPICE OF LIFE
Variety is the watchword in guest-room layouts in the new Claude Pratte Wing. Some rooms have regular windows; some have dormers. On the floor above the health club, rooms are long and deep, each with a sitting area and a sleeping area. Higher up, the exterior walls are much closer to the corridors, so rooms are narrow and wide. All the rooms in the new wing are large, and corner rooms have the added advantage of good views over the rooftops of Quebec; some incorporate circular turret spaces (above).
Photographs by Denis Farley.

Elévation rue Mont-Carmel

Hôtels et Villégiatures Canadien Pacifique

Le Château Frontenac

agrandissement de l'aile Mont-Carmel

JUST ADD 50 YEARS
The designers decided to match the exterior
materials and design elements of the existing
historic portions of the hotel in the addition; in
a few decades weathering will blur the
distinction between new and old. The roof of
the addition (center of photograph left,
left   side of elevation drawing above) is the
same design as the historic roofs and picks up
the main ridge line of the existing Mont Carmel
Wing, which it adjoins. The new roofing is
copper; time will give it the same green patina
seen on the copper of the main tower (left side
of photograph).
Photograph by Denis Farley; drawing by
Le Groupe Arcop.

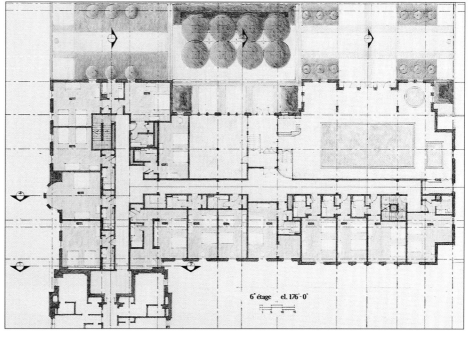

6° étage   el. 176'-0'

NOOKS AND CRANNIES
The brick and limestone exterior of the addition match the materials of the older portions of the building as closely as using current building materials can. The limestone banding on the walls extends the design of the existing building — as do the floor levels on the interior. The stone facing on the lower portion of the parking garage below the addition already existed, but the brick and stone design above it was added during the renovation to disguise ventilation openings as windows. Most of the details in the addition are based on ones from the original building, but others like the crenellations of the parapet around the new roof terrace (left) were created anew for the addition.
Photographs by Denis Farley.

THE SPA THAT CAME IN FROM THE COLD
Wintertime visitors who don't like the cold have a swimming pool, a wading pool and a whirlpool spa to console them in the new health club (above). A work-out room, massage rooms and a steam room are available to those who get waterlogged, and during good weather, the outdoor terrace next to the pool gives the health club an open-air feeling (left).
Photographs by Brigitte Ostiguy.

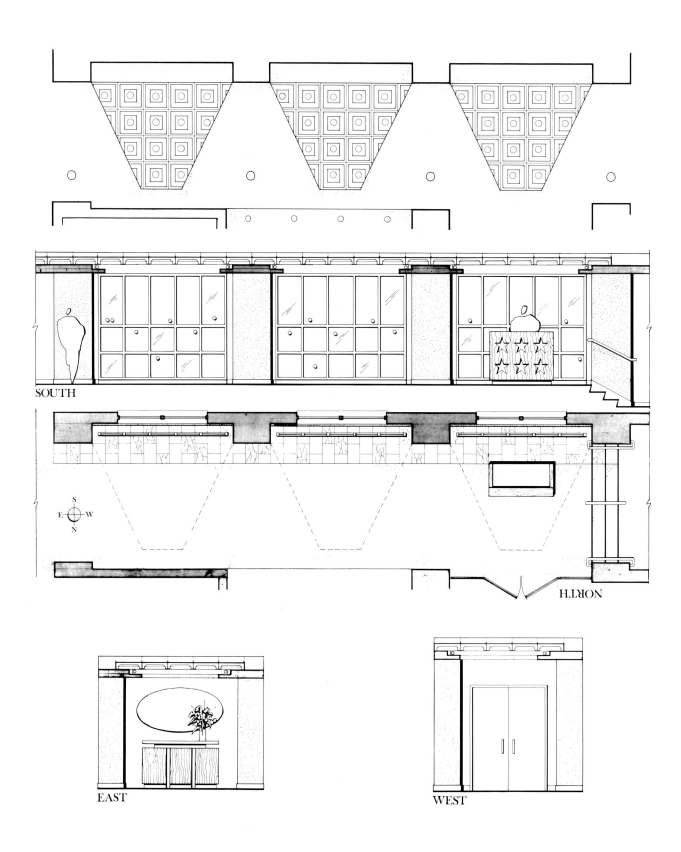

SOUTH

NORTH

EAST

WEST

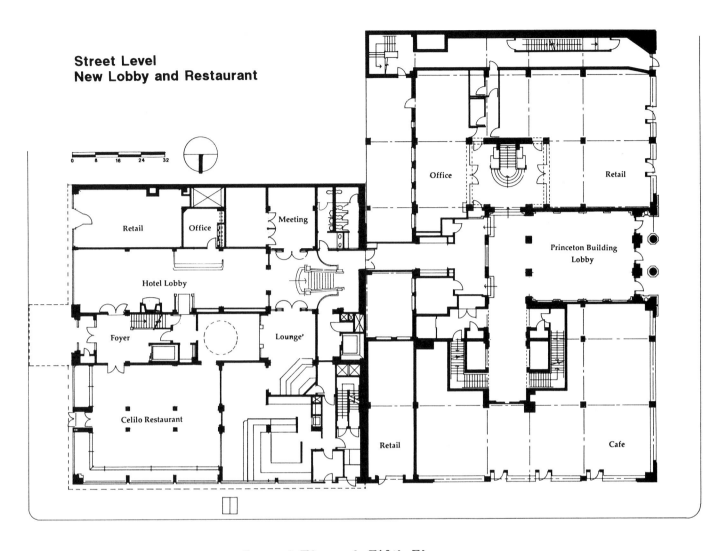

**Street Level
New Lobby and Restaurant**

0 8 16 24 32

Retail

Office

Meeting

Hotel Lobby

Foyer

Lounge'

Celilo Restaurant

Retail

Office

Retail

Princeton Building
Lobby

Cafe

Second Through Fifth Floors
Partial Plan

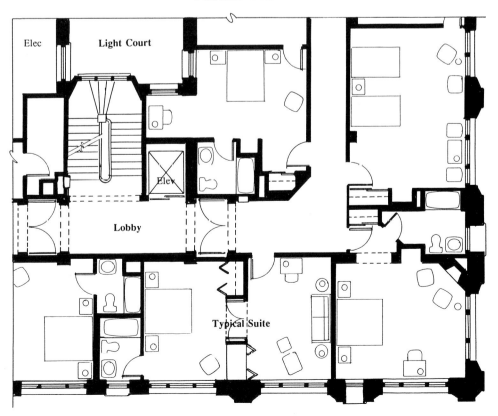

Elec

Light Court

Elev

Lobby

Typical Suite

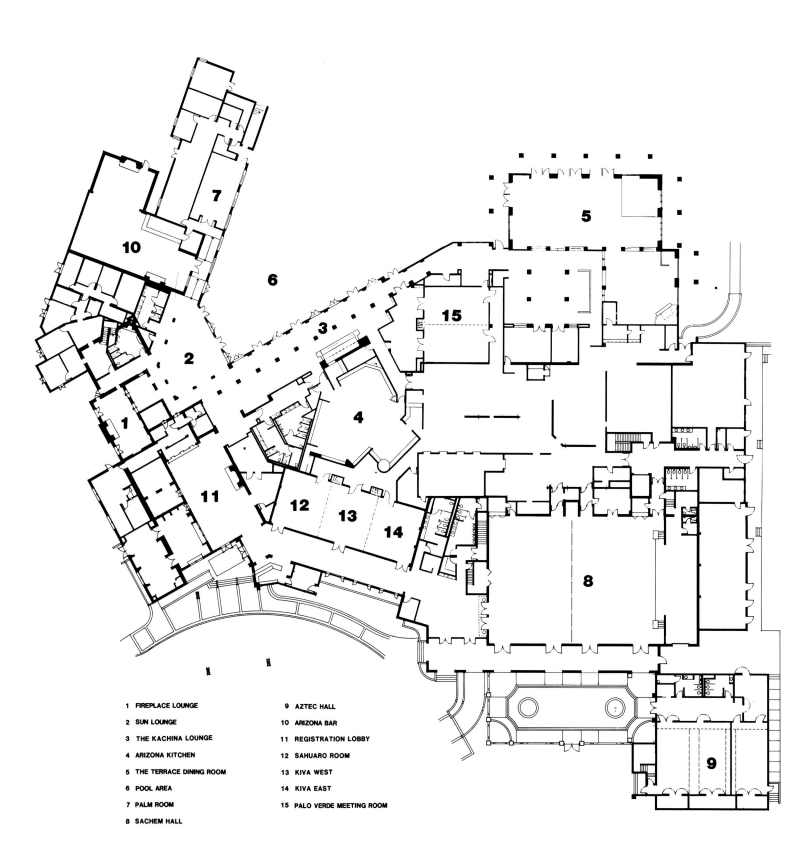

1 FIREPLACE LOUNGE

2 SUN LOUNGE

3 THE KACHINA LOUNGE

4 ARIZONA KITCHEN

5 THE TERRACE DINING ROOM

6 POOL AREA

7 PALM ROOM

8 SACHEM HALL

9 AZTEC HALL

10 ARIZONA BAR

11 REGISTRATION LOBBY

12 SAHUARO ROOM

13 KIVA WEST

14 KIVA EAST

15 PALO VERDE MEETING ROOM

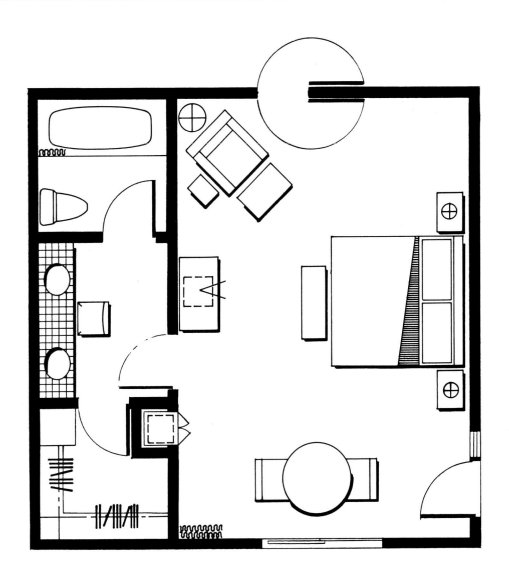

GUESTROOMS

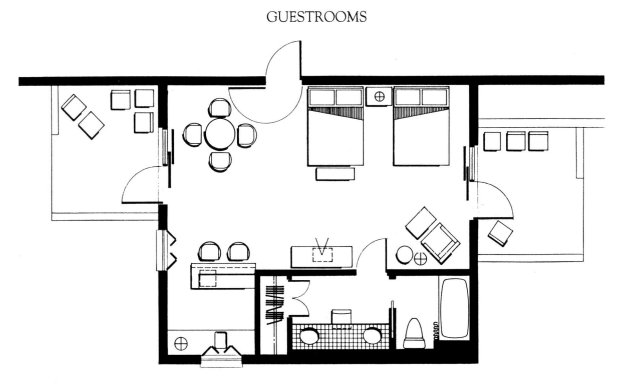

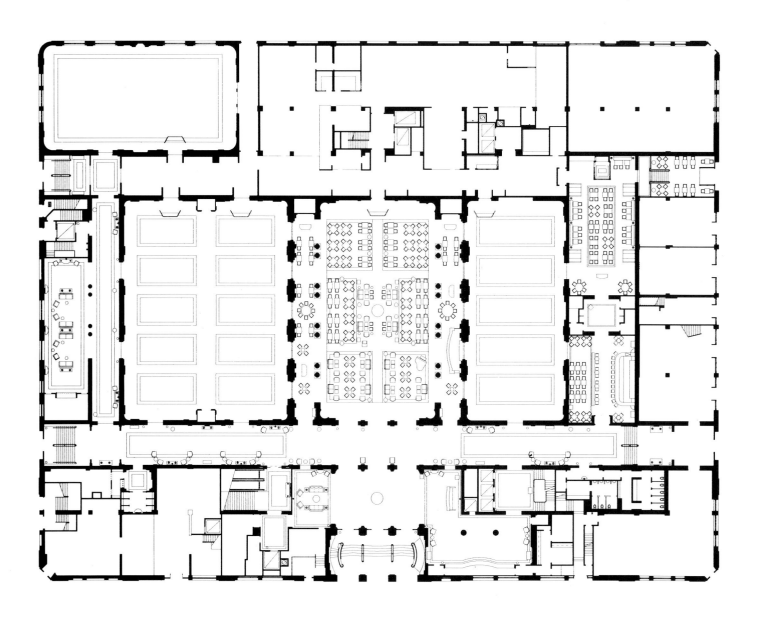

Ground Floor Plan

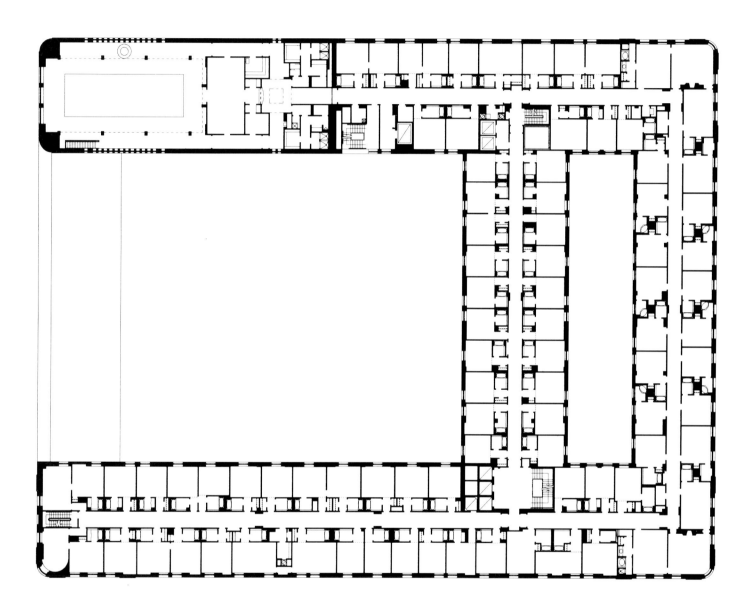

Fourth Floor Plan